The Heart Of Cleveland
Public Square In The 20th Century

By

Gregory G. Deegan

&

James A. Toman

PUBLISHING INFORMATION

Copyright © 1999
Cleveland Landmarks Press, Inc.
All Rights Reserved

First Edition
First Printing

ISBN - 0-9376760-12-5

Library of Congress Number - 99-074779

Published by
Cleveland Landmarks Press, Inc.
13610 Shaker Boulevard, Suite 503
Cleveland, Ohio 44120-1592

Design by
Moonlight Publishing
Rusty Schneider, Jr.
Hinckley, Ohio

Printed by Phillips Brothers, Inc.
Springfield, Illinois

Acknowledgments

After our last book, *Cleveland Stadium: The Last Chapter,* went on sale in July 1997, we had the opportunity to talk with most of the booksellers in the Greater Cleveland area. As we chatted with them, they would frequently ask, "What is your next project?" At the time we had not yet given that much thought, but we were intrigued by hearing them comment that customers looking for a Cleveland book most often asked about a book on the Terminal Tower or Tower City or Public Square. Cleveland Landmarks Press's first title, *The Terminal Tower Complex,* was published in 1980 and was long out of print. So as we considered our next venture and as we thought about the changing of the century, we came to the conclusion that Public Square, as the symbolic heart of the Greater Cleveland community, made great sense as the focus for our next project. We thank our bookselling friends for planting the idea.

During our research, many people were of real help to us. We wish to thank the following: our partners in Cleveland Landmarks Press, Dan and Cathy Cook; our designer, Rusty Schneider; Bill Becker, Cleveland State University archivist; Bill Barrows, Cleveland State University special collections librarian; Mary Perencevic from Cleveland Public Library's Cleveland Photograph Collection; Chris Wood of Cleveland Public Library's history department; Robert Keller, Drew Rohlik, Will Voegele, Ellen Koonce, Anthony McVery, and Sheree Warner of Tower City Center; Robert Keiser from the Cleveland Landmarks Commission; Bill McLaughlin of the City of Cleveland's Department of Engineering; and to Joe Vargas of Lorain County Community College.

We are also grateful to our friend and colleague Blaine Hays for sharing his wonderful Cleveland photo collection with us; likewise we thank our long-time friends, Cleveland photograph experts Bruce Young and Jim Spangler, for their help with selection and reproduction; and we thank David Kachinko for his aerial photos on the front and back covers and on the title page. We appreciate as well the help of Julie Demorest of the Cleveland Orchestra. A hearty thanks to John Yasenosky for putting together our two maps of the Public Square neighborhood.

And finally, a special word of appreciation to some special people for their support and patience while we were immersed in our Public Square labors: thanks Liz and Katie.

Gregory G. Deegan
James A. Toman
September 1999

The Heart of Cleveland

Introduction

Ask a Greater Clevelander to list some places that come to mind when she or he thinks of downtown, and the lists will vary. Some lists will begin with the Terminal Tower, Cleveland's most famous landmark. Or perhaps the younger generation will instead refer to the complex as Tower City Center, thinking primarily of the popular shopping mall that was developed out of the former Cleveland Union Terminal. Or these same people might mention the Flats, the city's nightlife district. Other more sports-minded folks might put Jacobs Field or Gund

1894 Proposal - - with a city hall on the northern two quadrants

Arena at the top of their lists, or even pencil in either the old or the new Cleveland Stadium. For theater lovers, the list would most likely be headed by Playhouse Square or by one of the theaters which make up the revitalized entertainment center. But while the top entry on the list may vary with the particular interest of the individual, on everyone's list, somewhere, will appear Public Square.

That the Square would be considered so important to Clevelanders might seem surprising. After all, it measures just under nine acres and makes up only a small fraction of the 77 square miles that comprise the city of Cleveland itself. The town's public park is an even more minute part of the Greater Cleveland metropolitan area. In terms of history, it would be a rare Clevelander who today would recognize the names of Seth

1945 Proposal - - **with new victory obelisks and no Soldiers and Sailors Monument**

1959 Proposal - - with a below-surface bus depot

Pease and Amos Spafford, the two Connecticut surveyors who laid out the green. Neither the size of the Square nor the story of its origin accounts for the significance which that parcel of land has had in the minds of Clevelanders and in the history of the town. There is much more to it than that.

The main reason why we chose to title this book *The Heart of Cleveland* is not because of mundane facts such as these, but because the Square is in the lifeblood of Cleveland. Since the city's founding, area residents have cherished their town's green, and though the years have now transformed it into a small patch at the hub of a sprawling metropolis, Greater Clevelanders have not lost the sense that the city's central acreage is a very special place.

It is our thought that the changes which have taken place in and around Public Square have mirrored in a real way the changing fortunes of the community itself. When the times were buoyed by optimism and determination, activity on and around the Square became vibrant. When the city entered into a time of drift or malaise, the Square began to look worn and tired. It is perhaps also important to note what did not emerge at the confluence of Superior Avenue and Ontario Street, for ideas that were rejected also are telling signs of what Clevelanders valued. That is another reason that we chose the title. The pulse of the city's life is, after all, but a reflection of the beating of its heart.

As Clevelanders enter upon the 21st century and look forward to what new wonders it will bring to the city and its citizens, it is likely that many will also look back and reflect on what took place during the century just ended. Apart from the inquiries of professional historians, though, these backward glances for most people can be neither extensive nor systematic. Their lives are filled with too many other daily demands to allow it to be otherwise.

So perhaps a quick glimpse at a century's happenings at the city's center, a metropolitan microcosm, will do. And so we chronicle some of those events, recognizing that our survey is both partial and lean. Some of the structures and events we describe have already passed out of living memory. Others will trigger for readers of a certain age actual remembrances of times past, some of these also soon to be the province of archivists rather than activists. Some are of recent vintage, their traces still green. Regardless, we hope our chronicle will be able to answer some questions about the past, refresh some fond but fading recollections, describe some of Cleveland's traditions over the last 100 years, and provide a brief but pleasant escape from the relentless pressures of the present.

For more than two centuries Clevelanders have diligently tried to protect the open space of their city's commons from commercial intrusion. On that cherished acreage they have mingled, mourned, celebrated, and commemorated. These countless Clevelanders have bequeathed to us something very special. We hope that when someone one day records the chronicle of the 21st century, she or he will be able to report that Clevelanders have continued to keep faith with the legacy of their forbearers and that Public Square has remained hallowed ground.

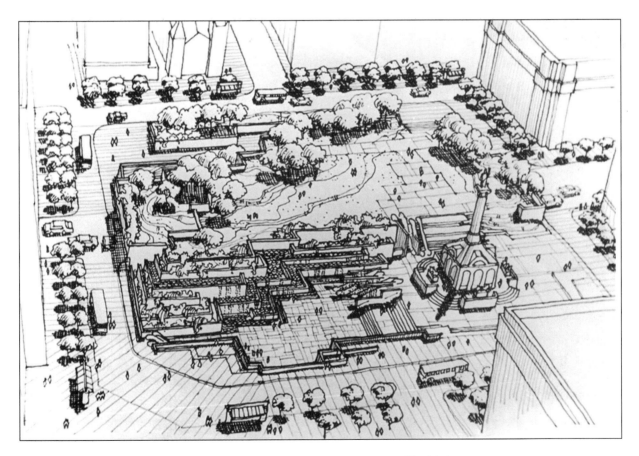

1962 Proposal - - with four quadrants rolled into one

The Heart of Cleveland

Prologue to the 20th Century

As Clevelanders counted down the last hours of the 19th century, they could not help but be optimistic about the future of their city. Spurred by the industrial needs of the Civil War, Cleveland in the last third of the century had become an industrial giant. Attracted by the employment opportunities, waves of Eastern European immigrants had made their way to the city, and the population skyrocketed. In 1900 Cleveland's population stood at 381,768. The city ranked seventh in the United States.

So Clevelanders put up with the smoke and smells of its industrial core, and they were not unduly concerned when on Sunday, December 31, 1899, an oil slick on the Cuyahoga River had burst into flames (and not for the last time) and the downtown skies were filled with smoke. The city's fire department rushed its hook and ladder truck, its pumpers and hose carts, and its fire tug to the scene, and the flames were extinguished. As the 20th century dawned, most Clevelanders were not much concerned with the ecological price that industrialization brought with it. For them, industry meant prosperity. The Cleveland *Plain Dealer* that day predicted "a great year for Cleveland" with much new construction and a host of business conventions.

As the clock chimed in the new century, Clevelanders welcomed it with the peeling of the city's church bells, and many attended special midnight church services, no doubt offering prayers that their city's prosperous times might continue.

Later on that January 1, 1900, morning, when Clevelanders awoke to the first light of the new century, they were greeted with clear skies but a temperature struggling to reach into the teens. While many no doubt took comfort in oven-warmed kitchens and fireplace-heated parlors, the more hearty souls were eagerly anticipating a trolley trip downtown to Public Square to witness marvelous new developments in travel technology.

On that New Year's Day, Public Square was once again serving as the backdrop for another of the many and varied events which perennially have enriched life in Cleveland. On January 1, 1900, the Square served as the starting and ending point for a parade of horseless carriages, a display of modern technology which its organizers felt well represented the emphasis that Cleveland ingenuity and enterprise would take in the dawning century. In fact Cleveland would indeed play a pivotal role in the approaching automotive age.

The horseless carriage parade route began at the northeastern quadrant of Public Square, adjacent to the Chamber of Commerce Building (now the site for Key Tower), and worked its way south to Euclid Avenue, then east to Erie Street (East Ninth), then to Prospect Street, west to Ontario Street, and then north back to the Square. The array of gasoline-, steam-, and electric-powered vehicles chugged, wheezed, and whirred their way along the parade route at a steady six miles per hour. The cold weather, however, did wreak some havoc. With the high temperature that New Year's day reaching only 16° Fahrenheit, the parade route had to be shortened. One balky vehicle still succumbed to the cold, catching fire as it reached Erie Street. The piles of snow on the ground proved a godsend for the frustrated driver.

The parade gave the onlookers a glimpse of the brave new world that the 20th century promised to bring, and as they waited on Public Square for their streetcars to take them back home, a glance about would surely have also offered ample evidence of the march of time and of Cleveland's growing momentum towards becoming one of America's great cities.

Adult Clevelanders in 1900 would have had to marvel at the changes that had taken place in the Public Square neighborhood over the previous decade. Those changes had clearly transformed its character from an old-fashioned New England town center to an urban park surrounded by ever taller towers of steel and stone.

Public Square was laid out in 1796-1797 by Seth Pease and Amos Spafford for the Connecticut Land Company expedition which Moses Cleaveland had led to the banks of the Cuyahoga River. Using the then-state-of-the-art measuring system of 66-foot chains to lay out the city, the surveyors followed typical New England practice and provided for an open town center. Cleveland's town center, its Public Square, consisted of 382,580 square feet, or 8.78 acres. Twelve lots were laid out along the perimeter of the Square. Superior Street cut through the Square from east to west, and Ontario Street bisected it from north to south. That street

Cuyahoga County's third court house was located on Frankfort Street, at the northwest corner of Public Square. Originally three stories when new in 1857, two more floors were added in 1884. *(Cleveland* Press *Collection of the Cleveland State University Libraries)*

layout led to the Square eventually assuming the character of four discrete quadrants.

In those early days the open town center proved an ideal grazing ground for the pioneer settlers' domestic livestock, and it was also around the Square's perimeter that prominent Clevelanders chose to build their homes. For the first third of its existence, Public Square's character remained bucolic and the area around it essentially residential. An early photograph even shows what seems to have been a homegrown baseball field occupying one of the Square's quadrants.

In 1858 the United States dedicated its Court House, Customs House, and Post Office on the northeast quadrant of Public Square at Superior Avenue. While this building gave way to a replacement in 1911, the federal courts continue to conduct business at that site. *(Ohio Historical Society)*

Yet as the growth of the city in terms of both population and commerce accelerated, pressures were ignited that would change Public Square from a rustic park to an urban hub and its immediate environs from a residential neighborhood to the city's commercial center. The city's early mercantile center, which had been centered in the Flats and along Water, Bank, and Seneca streets (West Ninth, Sixth, and Third streets in what today is known as the Warehouse District) had become densely packed, and blocked by the Cuyahoga River to the west, the only direction available to accommodate the pent-up need for expansion was to the east, towards Public Square. And though some residents and traditionalists fought the incursion of commercial interests to the Public Square area, by the middle of the 19th century, the outcome of that battle was clearly tilting toward the interests favored by the business community.

Even early on, however, Public Square was not entirely surrounded by residential property, nor was the Square itself devoid of all buildings. For some 43 years, parts of Public Square were occupied by county court houses. The first court house was built in 1815 within the northwest quadrant. In 1826 it was replaced by a larger facility, this time located in the southwest quadrant. An accompanying jail was located where today the Terminal Tower stands. Those facilities were also soon taxed by overcrowding, and plans were drawn for a third county court and detention facility. That third court house was built at Frankfort Street and the Square's northwest quadrant (where the 55 Public Square Building is now located). It was connected to a jail house built at Seneca Street and Frankfort. When the new court house opened in 1857, the old building in the southwest quadrant was razed.

One year later, in 1858, on the former Leonard Case property, facing the northeast quadrant of the Square between Superior and Rockwell streets, federal authorities dedicated a new court house, as well as a customs house and post office building of their own (the federal court house that now occupies that site replaced the earlier structure in 1911).

One of the earliest non-residential developments along the Square, facing the southwest quadrant at Superior Street, was Mowrey's Tavern, which opened in 1815. In 1835 that property became the site of travelers' lodging. It was first occupied by the Cleveland House and then by the Dunham House. In 1852 a new five-story brick Forest City House replaced the earlier hotels. The large new hotel was soon in earnest competition with the Weddell House on Bank Street for recognition as the city's premier hotel.

Another early non-residential use at Public Square was for a house of worship. In 1820 early Clevelanders chartered the First Presbyterian Church, and in 1834 they chose Public Square to be the front yard for their new sanctuary. It was the first church in the city to be built from stone. The grey sandstone building faced the northwest quadrant of Public Square at Ontario Street. The original church building was replaced with a larger stone edifice on the same site in 1855. Its 228-foot steeple made the new church visible from a considerable distance. While that original steeple succumbed to fire in 1857, the structure of the church building, though damaged, survived, and its interior was rebuilt. Better known to the Cleveland community as Old Stone Church, it is Public Square's oldest extant structure.

The site on the southwest quadrant of Public Square at Superior Avenue has been the location of a hotel ever since 1815. The Forest City House held that position from 1852 until 1916. *(Bruce Young Collection)*

By mid-century commercial blocks were also intruding on plots formerly occupied by residences. In 1854 the three-story Chapin Block opened at the southeastern edge of the Square at Euclid Avenue, and the Hoffman Block opened on the southeastern quadrant at Superior Street. Plans for two other major institutional moves were also in the works. That same year, the City of Cleveland moved its administrative headquarters into the Jones Block, another new office structure on the southwestern edge of the Square. The city offices remained in that location until 1876 when they moved to the Case Block at Superior and Wood streets (where today the Cleveland Public Library's main building stands).

Perhaps it was the fact that the new county court house would make it possible to rid the Square of all buildings. Perhaps it was the commercial or institutional replacements which were replacing most of the homes which had ringed the Square. Whatever the cause, by 1852 an organized citizens' campaign was underway to guarantee the preservation of Public Square as a public park. Voters were asked to sign petitions to the city government, demanding that Public Square be kept free of any further commercial intrusion. The petitions represented the first skirmish in what would soon become a battle to define the future character of Public Square. That struggle began in earnest in 1856 and lasted until 1867. It has come to be known as the Public Square Fence War.

Public Square was a peaceful place, despite the presence of a cannon from the Civil War. This scene of the northeast quadrant also shows the rostrum/reviewing stand in the background. The old U. S. Court House is to the right. *(Cleveland* **Press** *Collection of the Cleveland State University Libraries)*

In 1856 to mark the Ohio State Fair held in Public Square that year and to celebrate the city's new water pumping system, the city fathers installed a large cast iron pool and fountain in the Square's center, where Superior Avenue and Ontario Street intersected. Though the fountain was located at the center point of the two roadways, its jetting waters did not unduly affect the limited amount of carriage traffic that then passed through the Square.

On November 25, 1856, however, a more significant deterrent was put into place. Those opposed to the encroachment of commerce into the Public Square area had succeeded in convincing Cleveland City Council to erect a fence around the perimeter of Public Square, effectively truncating Superior and Ontario streets at the Square's outer boundary, and forcing traffic to detour around the Square via the marginal roadways. When the city's first horse-drawn streetcars began operating in 1859, like the conveyances of individuals, they were forced to detour around the Square rather than travel through it. Their tracks were laid along the southwestern perimeter of the Square to connect Ontario Street with the West Superior business district.

Inside the white wooden fence line, the four quadrants of the Square became a traffic-free zone. On September 5, 1860, a monument to Admiral Oliver Hazard Perry, hero of the 1813 Battle of Lake Erie, was installed on the Square. Sculpted in marble by Cleveland artist William

Walcutt, it was situated in the same location previously occupied by the central fountain. A crowd estimated at about 100,000 filled the Square to witness the monument's dedication. In 1861 the traditionalists lobbied Cleveland City Council to change the name of Public Square to Monumental Park. Council agreed to the name change on April 16, 1861. And while the new name, along with the "Public Square" designation, would appear on city plat maps for another 71 years, for most Clevelanders the name "Public Square" was already too deeply etched to be erased by political decree. Aside from official documents, Public Square remained just that in popular parlance.

Public Square has long been the city's main repository for monuments. Here the Commodore William Hazard Perry monument occupies the center of the Square, a position it occupied until 1878. The First Presbyterian Church (Old Stone) is in the background. *(Cleveland* Press *Collection of the Cleveland State University Libraries)*

The Perry monument was moved several times. Here it rests on the southeast quadrant of the Square. The cannon commemorates Perry's 1813 victory. *(Cleveland Picture Collection of Cleveland Public Library)*

The traditionalists' efforts to preserve the Public Square area from what they perceived as the covetous grasp of the Warehouse District's commercial interests ultimately brought only a short reprieve. The city's business leaders had resented the inconvenience caused by the fenced-in square, and they lobbied Cleveland City Council to reopen the streets. When their pleas proved unavailing, the business leaders turned to the courts to seek relief from what they felt had been an illegal closing of dedicated roadways. On August 21, 1867, Cleveland Municipal Court ruled in their favor, and three days later, the fences came down, the Perry monument notwithstanding.

For the next 11 years the Perry statue remained in the Superior-Ontario intersection, but as traffic increased, city officials decided that safety required its relocation. In 1878 it was moved to a position in the southeast quadrant just south of its center point, and traffic through the Square began to flow more freely. At the time Superior Street was 132 feet wide, and Ontario Street was 96 feet wide. The Square was then ringed by the North, East, South, and West roadways, as well as intersected by the two main streets. The surface of the streets was Medina Block stone. If the square footage occupied by the roadways around and through the Square is subtracted from the original plot, the actual acreage of Public Square green space was actually reduced to 4.38 acres.

The end of the Fence War signaled the beginning of the final transformation of Public Square into the city's new commercial center. In 1867 the Society for Savings Bank, which had begun its life in the Warehouse District in 1849, opened its new three-story headquarters at 127 Public Square, at the eastern edge of the Square's northeast quadrant (where the Key Tower stands today). And there it grew. Today, in its modern incarnation as Key Bank, the financial institution ranks as Public Square's third oldest resident (after the First Presbyterian Church and the federal government).

In 1868 First Presbyterian Church replaced the steeple which had been destroyed by the 1857 fire. The second steeple, however, only survived until 1884 when another fire struck.

Across the Square where Euclid Avenue begins, was the homestead and offices for the Cushing father-son medical team. The father, Erastus Cushing, had built his home and started medical practice there in 1835, where he was later joined in the practice by his son Henry. In 1870, however, the Cushings tore down their former home and erected a four-

By 1867 the Society for Savings had outgrown its home in the Warehouse District and moved to the northeast quadrant of Public Square. It occupied this site until 1890. *(Bruce Young Collection)*

Scaffolding enfolds the eastern tower of the Old Stone Church. To the west are the Wick Block, which contained the Lyceum Theater, and the Cuyahoga County Court House. *(Cleveland Picture Collection of Cleveland Public Library)*

story building in its place. The Cushing Block was where John D. Rockefeller in 1870 opened the first office for his newly incorporated Standard Oil Company (Ohio).

At the same time a new dry goods firm was looking for a place in the Warehouse District to open its business. The Cushings convinced Taylor, Kilpatrick and Company to try Public Square instead. The business took what at that time was a risk, opening a commercial venture so far from the rest of the business district. The company moved into a portion of the Cushing Block's first floor, at 120-124 Public Square. The risk soon turned out to have been well taken, and the business rapidly grew. In 1886 William Taylor bought out his partner's share of the business and renamed it William Taylor Son and Company. Expanding its selection of merchandise, Taylor's (as it was generally known) soon occupied the entire four-story building, and Public Square had gained its first department store. The William Taylor Son and Company development is generally viewed as the beginning of the commercial era for the Square.

Four years later another retail operation became a Taylor's neighbor. A home furnishings store, Beckwith, Sterling & Company, moved from the Warehouse District to the building just east of Taylor's on Euclid Avenue. In 1889 the company changed its name to Sterling, Welch & Company (later to be known as Sterling Lindner Davis and finally as Sterling Lindner). Both the Sterling and Taylor stores would later move farther east on Euclid Avenue and have long and successful business lives. Their early presence on the Square, however, helped cement the Square's retail future.

Various other two- three- and four-story commercial buildings were also built around the Square's perimeter. One of those three-story buildings, however, brought something different to Public Square. The Wick Block, home to the banking firm of Henry Wick and Company, was built on the northwest quadrant of the Square in 1883, with the County Courthouse as its neighbor to the west and the Old Stone Church its neighbor to the east. Besides the offices, the Wick Block also was home to the Park Theater. Its premier performance, on October 22, 1883, featured a classic comedy, Richard Sheridan's *School for Scandal*. In 1889 the theater space was renovated, and it reopened as the Lyceum Theater.

Perhaps those who had fought the good fight against the commercialization of Public Square were not entirely unsuccessful. An emerging consensus was that Public Square itself must be preserved as an urban park. In 1871 the City of Cleveland established a Board of Park Commissioners to oversee the city's green spaces. The following year the City established a $5,000 fund for the beautification of the Square, and it later authorized a $30,000 bond issue to complete the work. All of the quadrants benefited from new plantings of shrubs and trees. In the southwest quadrant a two-level pond with a fountain and a waterfall was excavated. A walkway from Superior to Ontario crossed over the pond by means of a small stone bridge. A model steamboat (now a part of the Western Reserve Historical Society collections) later plied the waters of the pond. The northeast quadrant gained a log pavilion and a sandstone rostrum/bandstand/reviewing stand at its eastern edge. The center of the northwest quadrant was graced with a fountain and small lily pond encircled by a wrought iron fence. The Perry monument continued as the focal point of the southeast quadrant. This was the first general renovation of Public Square itself.

By 1885 the Square was filled by modest office and commercial blocks, but these largely undistinguished structures were not destined to survive too long in a city that was rapidly growing. Cleveland was poised to follow in the footsteps of Chicago and New York in embracing the skyscraper as the quintessential symbol of urban prosperity.

The skyscraper era for Public Square began in 1889 when the Society for Savings Bank commissioned the prominent Chicago architectural firm of Burnham and Root to design a new headquarters building on land immediately to the west of its existing building. Once occupied by the Clark homestead and more recently by a Chinese laundry and Turkish bath, part of Cleveland's first "Chinatown" neighborhood, the Ontario and Public Square site soon attracted a steady stream of sidewalk superintendents as the stone and steel edifice began to rise. Not truly a skyscraper since its weight is not supported by an interior steel skeleton but rather by its massive exterior granite and sandstone walls, the building nonetheless looked like a skyscraper as it rose to ten stories and 152 feet. As was common in those early days of the high rise, the upper floors of the building were built around a central light court. The central open space provided light and ventilation and helped backlight the stained glass-ornamented ceiling of the ornate first-floor banking lobby. The Society for Savings Building was Cleveland's tallest building when it opened on June 23, 1890.

The Burnham and Root building was the start of a trend to surround Public Square with tall buildings. In 1892 ground was broken for the seven-story Cuyahoga Building (originally named the Parmalee Building), another product of the Burnham and Root firm. It was the first Cleveland office building to have a structural steel interior. It replaced the Hoffman Block. The next building to cast its shadow over the Square was the 1895 Mohawk Building, located at Frankfort Avenue and the northwest quadrant of the Square (this

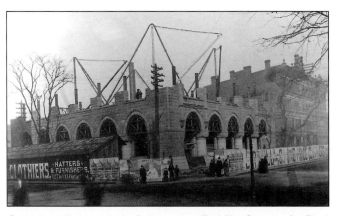

Construction got underway on Public Square's first "skyscraper" in 1889. At their base the walls of the new headquarters for the Society for Savings were five feet thick.   (Cleveland Press Collection of the Cleveland State University Libraries)

The Society for Savings Building nears completion in 1890. The bank building briefly held the title of the city's tallest structure, at 10 stories and 152 feet. (Cleveland Press Collection of the Cleveland State University Libraries)

In 1896 the Society for Savings Building welcomed a new neighbor. The Cleveland Chamber of Commerce Building occupied the northeast quadrant site for 57 years. *(Cleveland Picture Collection of Cleveland Public Library)*

building had many name changes; it was later known as American Trust, Ulmer, Public Square, and eventually as the 33 Public Square Building). Designed by Cleveland architect Charles Schweinfurth, it contained 14 floors.

In 1898, on the site of the Society for Savings' original Public Square home, which had most recently been home to the Western Reserve Historical Society, construction began on a new headquarters for the Cleveland Chamber of Commerce (now the Greater Cleveland Growth Association). Designed by the Boston firm of Peabody and Stearns, the seven-story neo-classical building was dedicated on May 2, 1899. Then in 1899 construction began on another neo-classical building, designed by George B. Post and Sons, at the southeastern quadrant of the Square and Euclid Avenue. The Williamson Building would replace a four-story predecessor which had been badly damaged by fire in 1897 and which itself had replaced the original Samuel Williamson homestead on the site. The new Williamson Building become the city's tallest at 16 stories when it opened in April 1900.

Not all the construction activity, however, was consigned to the perimeter of Public Square. In 1894 Public Square itself was the recipient of the most dramatic change in its history. In 1879 a committee of Civil War veterans had proposed a monument to honor the 10,000 local men who

In 1898 the statue of Victory atop the central column of the Soldiers and Sailors Monument looks down at the fountain on the Square's northeast quadrant. The tall structure behind the Civil War column is the clock tower for the Hull and Dutton store on Ontario Street. *(Cleveland Picture Collection of Cleveland Public Library)*

had served in the Union forces during the war, and the committee expressed its earnest recommendation "that the Monument be located in the center of Monumental Park, in the City of Cleveland." Not everyone was in favor of that location since the structure would significantly alter the Square's park-like setting. The Ohio legislature had approved the Soldiers' and Sailors' Monument Building Commission's plan, but opponents, with the full backing of the city, went to court to protect the Public Square setting from encroachment by the Commission. The case eventually made its way to the Ohio Supreme Court, which in 1892 ruled that Public Square belonged not to the City of Cleveland, but to the people in general, and that the legislature had the right to act in their name to authorize the Commission's plan.

The Soldiers and Sailors Commission turned to Clevelander Levi Scofield to design the Civil War memorial. His efforts resulted in the Victorian-style structure that eventually rose on the site. Scofield positioned the Soldiers and Sailors Monument on an elevated stone terrace located at the center of the southeast quadrant. Four diagonal pathways, interspersed by small sections of lawn, led up to the terrace. Occupying the center of the terrace was a granite mausoleum (the structure's interior space is called the tablet room; the names of the serving veterans are inscribed on its panels). Scofield surrounded the central structure's plaza with four bronze statuary groups mounted on stone bases. He topped the monument itself with a central column carrying a stylized statue of Victory and rising 125 feet above the southeast quadrant.

Building the Soldiers and Sailors Monument on Public Square meant that the Perry Monument once again had to be moved. It was relocated to Wade Park (then in 1913 it was again moved, this time to Gordon Park; then in 1929 it was replaced by a bronze replica, which in 1991 was brought downtown to Cleveland's Huntington Park on Lakeside Avenue). The decision of the court and the construction of the Soldiers and Sailors Monument also resulted in the City of Cleveland losing all control over the southeast quadrant.   The care of that quadrant and the monument was made the responsibility of the Commission, and then later that responsibility devolved to Cuyahoga County, which remains in control to the present time.

Thousands of Clevelanders attended the Civil War memorial's dedication ceremonies on July 4, 1894. Ohio Governor William McKinley presided over the rain-soaked ceremonies, which included a six-hour parade of sodden but intrepid marchers passing the Public Square reviewing stand.

Throughout the century, Public Square was the gathering site for Clevelanders' celebrations. Here, temporary stands in front of a decorated Society for Savings Building help hold a crowd that overflows the northeast quadrant. *(Cleveland* Press *Collection of the Cleveland State University Libraries)*

The placement of the Soldiers and Sailors monument solidified the place of Public Square as the civic center of the city. Although the tall new buildings that had been rising around Public Square's edges helped architecturally to define the Square's urban character, it was the uses that the Cleveland community made of the Square that cemented its role as the real heart of the city, the premier place where Clevelanders gathered to commemorate historic events and to celebrate special occasions.

The Soldiers and Sailors Monument on the southeast quadrant of Public Square is new in 1895. The view looks south from the roof of the Society of Savings Building. *(Cleveland Picture Collection of Cleveland Public Library)*

Over the course of the 19th century the events that drew Cleveland citizens to Public Square were both numerous and diverse. They ranged in solemnity from fairs to funerals, but probably the most common were events commemorating or celebrating civic holidays and martial triumphs.

Independence Day 1858 provides a good illustration. A crowd of about 40,000 Clevelanders gathered on the Square to watch a parade, and later many of them stayed on to share a picnic dinner, with lemonade served by the Total Abstinence Society. After the victuals were consumed, the crowd remained to marvel at a daring manned-balloon ascent.

On April 14, 1865, thousands of Clevelanders gathered in Public Square to celebrate the Union Army's victory in the Civil War. Events included a thanksgiving prayer service in the Old Stone church, a regimental parade, and plenty of cannon fire. That evening the Square was lighted by bonfires, but only two weeks later, the mood was much more somber as the city paid tribute to the country's slain president. Abraham Lincoln's body, on its way westward for burial in Illinois, arrived in Cleveland and was brought from the Euclid Avenue railroad station to rest in a pavilion next to the Perry statue in Public Square. A throng estimated at 100,000 came to the Square to pay their respects to the fallen leader and file past the catafalque.

Thousands of Clevelanders paid tribute to Abraham Lincoln in 1865 when the fallen president's body was brought to Public Square. The pavilion rests in the middle of Superior Avenue. *(Cleveland Press Collection of the Cleveland State University Libraries)*

In 1871 German-American Clevelanders decorated Public Square to celebrate their native land's victory in the Franco-Prussian War. The Perry Monument is at the right. *(Cleveland Picture Collection of Cleveland Public Library)*

In 1871 the large Cleveland German community celebrated their former homeland's triumph in the Franco-Prussian War. A two-mile parade made its way to Public Square where it passed through a triumphal arch installed to mark the German victory. The following year two cannons, one from the War of 1812 and the other from the Civil War, were added to the northeast quadrant of the Square, testimonials to military triumphs closer to home. In 1875 another balloon ascent marked Public Square Independence Day ceremonies.

Public Square was the scene for another kind of modern achievement when on the evening of April 29, 1879, Cleveland inventor Charles F. Brush established the viability of electric street lighting. He had hung 12 of his arc lamps on 150-foot poles around the Square to demonstrate the superiority of electric lighting over gas lamps. A sizeable crowd had gathered to witness the experiment. They were greatly impressed when Brush threw the switch and the Square was bathed in a steady electric glow. Equally impressed was Cleveland City Council, which authorized the installation of the lighting system throughout much of the downtown area. Cleveland became the first city anywhere to benefit from electric street lighting.

In 1881 President James A. Garfield, a native of Mentor, Ohio, fell to an assassin's bullet, and his body was returned to his home ground where it lay in state on Public Square beginning on September 24. Over the next three days approximately 100,000 Clevelanders paid their respects. Following services on the Square on September 26, the cortege left Public Square and proceeded to Lakeview Cemetery where the president's body was interred in a temporary crypt (the Garfield Monument there was not completed until 1890).

In 1888 Public Square gained another new monument. On July 23 Cleveland's Early Settlers Association commemorated Moses Cleaveland by installing a statue of the city's founder on the Square's southwest quadrant. Five hundred members of the association were present for the installation. Designed by James Hamilton, the life-sized bronze statue was positioned atop a granite plinth. Because the pond occupied the center ground of the quadrant, the statue was positioned towards its northeast corner, near Superior Street, facing towards the Superior/Ontario intersection.

These somber-colored arches in Public Square were erected for the funeral services of President James A. Garfield in September 1881. Following the services, the slain leader's body was taken to Lakeview Cemetery. *(Cleveland Picture Collection of Cleveland Public Library)*

Public Square received a second demonstration of the usefulness of electric technology on May 19, 1889. On that day, the first streetcar of Tom L. Johnson's Brooklyn and Southside Street Railway's West 14th Street line made its way to Public Square powered by 600 volts of direct current from an overhead wire grid. On July 7 electric-powered streetcars from the East Cleveland Street Railway Company's Euclid Avenue line also reached Public Square. The electric cars greatly speeded public transportation, and though some Clevelanders were at first wary of danger from the possible collapse of the overhead power lines, that apprehension soon faded.

The advent of the electrification of the street railway system eventually established Public Square as the city's local transportation hub. Each of the Square's four quadrants came to serve as ideal turning loops for the streetcar lines which converged on downtown from the various city neighborhoods. Public Square was soon marked by gleaming ribbons of crisscrossing steel tracks and an intricate overhead wire installation. The electric lines eased travel to downtown, and that convenience further solidified the role of the center city as the area's shopping mecca.

Though Cleveland was rapidly growing into a major metropolis, in 1894 it still was conducting city business from rented office space in the Case Block at East Third Street and Superior Avenue. The City fathers, however, had been considering Public Square as the site for a new city hall for some time, as 1870 sketches for a building on the Square show. Another

Public Square would look very different today had this 1894 proposal for a new Cleveland City Hall gone forward. But widespread concern to keep the Square an open space halted the project. *(Cleveland* Press *Collection of the Cleveland State University Libraries)*

quarter century passed, however, before concrete steps were taken to build the municipal building. In 1894 the city asked for and received permission from the Ohio legislature to use the northeast quadrant of "Monumental Park" for a new city hall, and voters approved funds to build the structure.

In April 1895 Cleveland City Council authorized funds for planning the new building, and Mayor Robert McKisson expressed the hope that construction would be far enough along that he would be able to lay the cornerstone on the city's centennial day in July 1896. The sketch for the new municipal headquarters revealed a monumental structure, planted right in the heart of Public Square. Designed by John Eisenmann, whose 1890 Arcade was then the city's most celebrated building, the mammoth Victorian edifice would have bridged Superior Avenue with a six-story structure, crowned with four five-story towers at each corner. Two shorter wings for the central building would have taken up most of the northeast and northwest quadrants. All that would be left of the quadrants' open space would be small lawns facing the east and west roadways.

On June 4 fences were installed around the northern quadrants to mark the construction site. The wooden barricades almost immediately set off warning bells. With one green quadrant already mostly lost to the Soldiers and Sailors Monument, the fences clearly indicated how little would be left of a green Public Square. Even the city's own Board of Park Commissioners raised objections, appealing on June 10 to City Council to "prevent the use of said park for other than park purposes." Two days later opponents went to court and gained an injunction against the construction. Prominent supporters of the injunction included the Chamber of Commerce, the Western Reserve Historical Society, the Society for Savings, and the Old Stone Church--all neighbors on the Square. As Cleveland historian William Ganson Rose described it, citizens were not apt to tolerate "trespassing upon Cleveland's historic front yard." To make sure that the City would not later succeed in having the injunction lifted, the coalition of neighbors then used its collective influence to get the Ohio Legislature to repeal its earlier authorization of the project. The idea of putting a city building in the Square was dead.

In 1896, however, the year of the city's centennial, Clevelanders were more than willing to welcome some other construction within the confines of the Square. A log cabin was built in the northeast quadrant directly in front of the Society for Savings Building. It served as a reception area for the centennial festivities. More significant was the construction of a giant commemorative arch. Built in the style of Paris's famous Arc de Triomphe, it stretched 120 feet across Superior Avenue, just east of Ontario Street, and towered 80 feet above street level.

In 1896 a towering wooden arch over Superior Avenue commemorated the centennial of the city's founding. In the rear, just in front of the bannered Society for Savings Building, is another centennial exhibit, a log cabin. *(Western Reserve Historical Society)*

Though its dimensions were impressive, the arch was built of wood and plaster, and thus Clevelanders were assured that when the centennial celebrations were over, it could be dismantled without too much delay. On July 22, the anniversary day of the city's founding, U.S. President Grover Cleveland threw a switch from his home in Massachusetts, and the arch was bathed by floodlights. A "Passing of the Century" parade then marched through the arch, to the great satisfaction of the thousands of Clevelanders who attended the event. Altogether, centennial festivities kept downtown and Public Square hopping from July 19 through July 30.

On July 10, 1898, Clevelanders joined in thanksgiving prayer services for the U. S. victory in the Spanish-American War. A cannon from that conflict was added to the Square's collection of military hardware.

Undoubtedly some of these events of the just completed century were recalled by the Clevelanders as they made their way home from the New Year's Day horseless carriage parade. It is likely that many of the citizens would also have come to think of the substantial buildings

Public Square has long been the central stop on the city's parade routes. Here marchers celebrate the nation's victory in the Spanish-American War. *(Cleveland Picture Collection of Cleveland Public Library)*

and familiar storefronts which were then ringing the Square as largely permanent fixtures. Yet of all the buildings surrounding the Square in 1900, only two (besides the Soldiers and Sailors Monument on the Square itself) would remain 100 years later. The landscape of Public Square itself would also undergo two major renovations in that same span of time.

One thing would remain constant, however. Public Square would continue to be the place where Clevelanders congregated for the meaningful rituals of civic life. Though much of the peripheral would indeed undergo major change, what was essential to the meaning of the Square would remain.

One hundred years later, Public Square would still beat as the heart of Cleveland.

At the 19th century's close, the Soldiers and Sailors Monument dominates the Public Square scene. The southwest quadrant forms the backdrop. *(Cleveland Picture Collection of Cleveland Public Library)*

A Progressive Era
1900 - 1919

The Progressive Era in the United States is typically described as reaching the peak of its influence and power in the 1890s, and continuing into the first decade of the 20th century. The era was a time of governmental reform, a period during which the earlier belief that the government which did the least was also that which was best was replaced by a new belief in the importance of governmental activism. In Cleveland the progressive spirit was suitably personified by Tom L. Johnson, Cleveland mayor from 1901 to 1909. In the minds of many Clevelanders the city's greatest mayor, Johnson is the only individual other than Moses Cleaveland to have a statue in his honor in Public Square.

Although operating under the constraints of an Ohio constitution which restricted local home rule, and which he decried as serving the interests of "Privilege," Johnson was undeterred from pursuing his objective of making the city better serve its citizens. His charisma and energy were such that he successfully set into motion many lasting changes in the way the city was governed and in the way the city looked. While perhaps best remembered for his long fight to wrest control over the local streetcar operation from private operators and place it into municipal hands, it was an effort in which he achieved only partial success. It was also during Johnson's administration that a Group Plan Commission was brought into being and given the responsibility to design for Cleveland a new governmental center, one that would fit the image of a great and thriving city.

Cleveland's need for a new city hall had not disappeared when the plans to build the Victorian pile on Public Square had been squelched by public outcry. Nor had the county's need for a new court house been met by the several additions which had been made to its 1857 structure on Public Square's northern edge. During the same time period the federal government was also looking to replace its antiquated 1858 Public Square court building, and the city's library was in need of a permanent and adequate home. To meet these needs, the Cleveland Chamber of Commerce had spearheaded a campaign to convince Clevelanders that

Cleveland's city hall was situated in rented space in the Case Block on Superior Avenue at East Third Street. The need for a permanent home was one of the factors that gave rise to the city's Group Plan. *(Cleveland Picture Collection of Cleveland Public Library)*

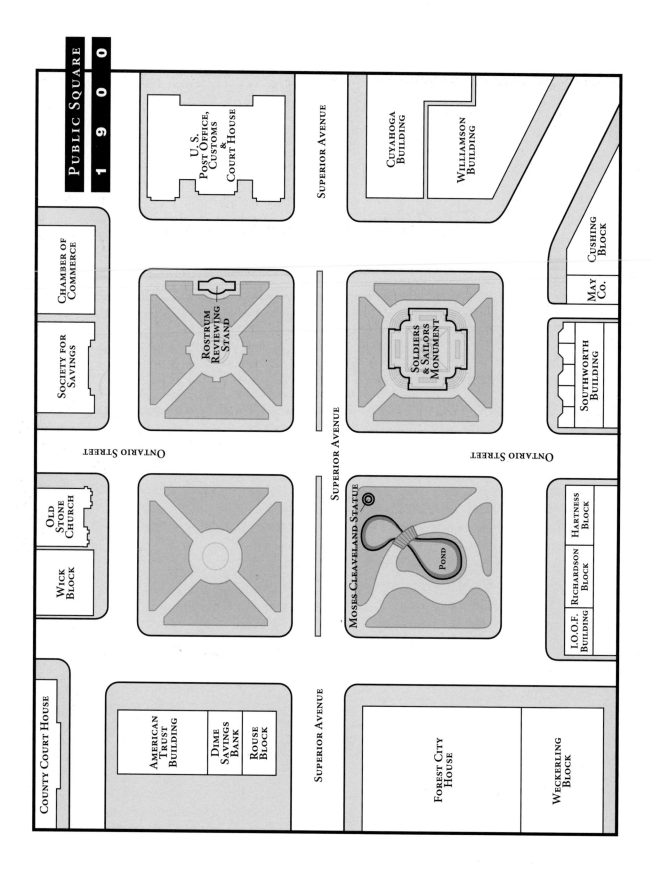

U.S. POST OFFICE, CUSTOMS & COURT HOUSE

SUPERIOR AVENUE

CUYAHOGA BUILDING

WILLIAMSON BUILDING

CUSHING BLOCK

CHAMBER OF COMMERCE

SOCIETY FOR SAVINGS

ROSTRUM REVIEWING STAND

SOLDIERS & SAILORS MONUMENT

MAY CO.

SOUTHWORTH BUILDING

ONTARIO STREET

ONTARIO STREET

OLD STONE CHURCH

WICK BLOCK

MOSES CLEAVELAND STATUE

POND

SUPERIOR AVENUE

HARTNESS BLOCK

RICHARDSON BLOCK

I.O.O.F. BUILDING

COUNTY COURT HOUSE

AMERICAN TRUST BUILDING

DIME SAVINGS BANK

ROUSE BLOCK

SUPERIOR AVENUE

FOREST CITY HOUSE

WECKERLING BLOCK

a governmental building program was not so much a drain on the public purse, but an opportunity to create for the city a civic center of lasting significance.

The Chamber's message was eventually heard in the state capital, and in 1902 the Ohio Assembly authorized the creation of a Group Plan Commission. Accordingly Ohio Governor George Nash established the commission, and on June 20 Mayor Johnson appointed to it three of the nation's foremost urban planners and architects, Daniel H. Burnham (one of the Society for Savings Building architects), Arnold R. Brunner, and John M. Carrere.

A little over one year later, on August 17, 1903, the commission unveiled its Group Plan design. The centerpiece of the design was be a 500-foot esplanade of green, stretching north from Rockwell Avenue and Wood Street (East Third) to the railroad tracks running along the lakefront. Along this Mall the plan called for a collection of new public buildings, all designed in a harmonious Beaux Arts neo-classical style. A new Cuyahoga County Court House and Cleveland City Hall would flank Mall C at Lakeside Avenue. Along the center section of the Mall (Mall B) would be three buildings. To its east would be a public auditorium for meetings and conventions. On the west side would be an exhibitions building and county administration building. At the southern end, along Mall A, would be a Cleveland Board of Education building, a Cleveland Public Library headquarters building, and a new federal court house. At the extreme northern end, the designers positioned a new union railroad station to replace the dilapidated 1859 depot located at the foot of Water (West Ninth) Street. The architects recommended that an element of the Society for Savings Building serve as a guide to the height of the new civic buildings. The arched windows on the bank building's sixth floor would set the upper limits for the new buildings.

The new U.S. Court House, Customs House and Post Office opened in 1911, the first of the Group Plan buildings to be completed. It replaced the 1858 federal building that had occupied the site. *(Cleveland* **Press** *photo, Jim Toman Collection)*

Construction on the first Group Plan building, the U. S. Post Office, Customs House, and Court House at Public Square's northeast quadrant and Superior Street, began in 1905, but a series of design changes delayed its completion until March 1911. Architect for the federal facility was Arnold Brunner, one of the Group Plan team members.

Planning and construction for the rest of the originally planned Mall buildings went on for the next 22 years, and even after that some further Group Plan-related work was carried out. Buildings from the original plan that were completed were: the Cuyahoga County Court House, designed by Lehman and Schmitt (1912); Cleveland City Hall, designed by J. Milton Dyer (1916); Public Auditorium, designed by Betts and McDowell (1922) and its Music Hall addition by Herman Kregelius (1927); Cleveland Public Library, designed by Walker and Weeks (1925); and the Cleveland Board of Education Building, also by Walker and Weeks (1930). The Mall green itself was not finally cleared of all the old structures on its grounds until 1933.

Besides giving the city a stately collection of public buildings of which Clevelanders were very proud, the Group Plan also added to the green space preserved in downtown Cleveland. The southwestern end of the Mall abuts the northeastern corner of Public Square and extends the city center's park-like setting towards the lakefront.

The Cuyahoga County Court House, which opened in 1912, made the old court house on the Square superfluous. It was the second building in the Group Plan to be completed. *(Cleveland* Press *Collection of the Cleveland State University Libraries)*

Despite the achievements of the Group Plan, its full complement of proposed buildings was not realized. The western edge of the Mall was not completed with the planned exhibition hall or county administration building (the current Cuyahoga County Administration Building was a 1956 project). Of greater significance to this story of Public Square, however, was that the plans for the lakefront railroad depot were also stymied. The truncation of the Mall Plan at the bluffs overlooking the lakefront may have left a void in the civic center design, but it created a need that a few years later would lead to Public Square's most impressive construction project.

But before the union station at Public Square would get onto the drawing boards, many other projects around the Square were brought from the planning stage to reality. The first decades of the 20th century were a time of many changes in the Square neighborhood.

In 1901 Cleveland Railway Company built four streetcar waiting rooms on Public Square. The northeast quadrant had two shelters. One faced the East Roadway, the other Superior Street. The Superior station also served as a visitors' information center. The southwest quadrant and the northeast quandrants' shelters faced Ontario Street. The southeast quadrant had no shelter. The wooden structures were soon nicknamed the Square's "pagodas" because their curving roof lines reminded people of Asian design. While the pagodas did provide waiting passengers with shelters, the streetcar operation at the time detracted from their utility. Streetcars were then looping around the Square's quadrants in counter-clockwise fashion so that the boarding doors faced away from the shelters. Patrons thus had to leave the shelters and walk around to the other side of the cars, exposing themselves to passing traffic, before they could board. This inconvenient system remained in effect until the loops were reversed during the 1930s.

By 1900 the area just south of Public Square, along Ontario Street, was becoming department store row. In 1899 David May bought the E. R. Hull & Dutton Company store on the east side of Ontario Street and introduced Clevelanders to the May Company. At the time, the building had six stories (with a clock tower above) and contained 73,000 square feet of space. Unfortunately, it had no Public Square frontage, unlike its older rival, the William Taylor Son and Company. May's motto was "Watch Us Grow," and from the very beginning the company pursued plans to have a Public Square frontage. It began to buy properties facing the Square along the South Roadway. (Although most people identify this stretch of street as Euclid Avenue, Euclid, which was not a part of the city's original street layout, actually begins at the eastern edge of the

As the 20th century dawned, almost all Clevelanders got to downtown by means of streetcar. In 1901 four of these stations were erected to give waiting passengers some shelter from the elements. People quickly nicknamed the shelters "pagodas." *(Blaine Hays Collection)*

When the May Company in Cleveland opened for business in 1899, its first location was in this Ontario Street store, just a couple of doors east of Public Square. The building previously had been home to the Hull & Dutton store. *(Cleveland* Press *Collection of the Cleveland State University Libraries)*

Located just across Public Square, to the left of the Soldiers and Sailors Monument column, in 1902 the May Company's new annex is under construction. The new building, which gave May's its greatly desired Square frontage, was just across an alleyway from its original store building. *(Cleveland* Press *Collection of the Cleveland State University Libraries)*

Square.) By 1902, the property transfers had taken place, and the May Company was able to open a six-story annex immediately east of Farnham Alley, at 22-24 Public Square. Both May Company buildings had entranceways on the alley, so shoppers could move between them with relative ease.

Two doors farther south on Ontario Street, at the corner of Prospect Street, another department store was also on the grow. Lewis A. Bailey had begun his dry goods business in 1881 from a small building on Prospect Street, just a few doors east of Ontario Street. In 1899 ownership of the store changed hands, and it became known as the Bailey Company. The new company's growth accelerated when it acquired the Cleveland Dry Goods Company on Ontario Street and added housewares and home furnishing departments. The expanded business needed both to consolidate and add to its selling space, and so Bailey's acquired the land at the corner of Ontario and Prospect streets. The site was then occupied by the old Prospect House inn. The inn was razed, and construction began on a large modern department store facility. Bailey's new seven-story building opened in 1903. Taylor's, Bailey's, and May's were then clustered close together. The W. P. Southworth Company, the city's largest grocer, was also located on Ontario Street, just a couple doors from the Square, and the Higbee Company, another department store founded in 1860, was operating from a building on Superior Street, just west of the Square. This concentration of retail space created the synergy during the first decade of the century which made the Public Square area the city's foremost shopping district, eclipsing the Warehouse District's former commercial prominence.

In 1904 another new office building made its debut on the Square. The Park Building, designed by Cleveland architect Frank S. Barnum, was constructed at the intersection of the South Roadway and Ontario Street, immediately west of Farnham Alley and the May Company annex. Its design was understated, the facade regular, modified only by the bay windows along the second and third floor levels. Its simplicity was in marked contrast to the elaborate design of the Chamber of Commerce Building across the Square from it. Containing a total of nine stories, the building offered street-level retail space with office accommodations on the floors above. Unlike its other and older cross-Square neighbor, the Society for Savings Building which underwent two major interior reconstructions over the years, the Park Building has retained most of its original interior design, and it therefore serves as Public Square's best example of turn-of-the-century office planning. Built for the Park Investment Company, an enterprise of the Truman Swetland family, major downtown developers during the early part of the century, the Park Building continues to by operated by the Swetland interests.

Public Square is alive with pedestrian and streetcar traffic in 1904. At the right the Park Building is under construction. The tall structure (left of center) is the Williamson Building, and adjacent to it is the Cuyahoga Building. *(Bruce Young Collection)*

In 1905 the City of Cleveland decided that because of the city's rapid growth, a more systematic way of identifying its streets was needed. The change largely involved giving the north-south streets numerical identifications. For example, Water Street became West Ninth, Bank Street became West Sixth, and Seneca Street became West Third. On the East Side, Wood Street became East Third, Sheriff Street became East Fourth, and Erie Street became East Ninth. At the same time Superior Street and Prospect Street were elevated to the status of avenues, joining Euclid which had been so designated in 1870. Ontario, however, remained a street.

By 1906 shoppers were coming to the Public Square area department stores in growing numbers, and soon the William Taylor Son and Company, which was occupying the oldest and the smallest store, decided that it needed to expand. Sufficient property in the area around the Square was not then available, so the company turned its eyes eastward along Euclid Avenue. The store purchased land at 630 Euclid Avenue, and in 1907 Taylor's moved from the Square to a new and large five-story building on Euclid (what is now the 668 Euclid Building). The Taylor move set in motion a whole series of department store developments.

In 1909 Sterling, Welch & Company followed the Taylor lead, moving from 12-14 Euclid Avenue to a new home at 1225-1239 Euclid Avenue, just east of East 12th Street. In 1910 the Higbee Company bought land at the northwest corner of East 13th Street and Euclid Avenue for a large new store. That same year, the Halle Brothers Company, which had begun business on West Superior Street in 1891 and in 1892 moved to the Nottingham Building on lower Euclid Avenue next to the Arcade, joined the move up the avenue. Its new 10-story building across the street from Sterling and Welch and the new Higbee store gave downtown Cleveland two department store hubs, one at Public Square (May's and Bailey's), the other on the western edge of what would become known as Playhouse Square. The smaller stores along the avenue between these two department store clusters benefited accordingly, as shoppers would walk "square to square" shopping along the avenue between the anchors.

The Bailey Company anchored the Ontario Street and Prospect Avenue corner just off Public Square. Along with Taylor's and May's, Bailey's helped make the Square area a shopping magnet. *(Cleveland Press Collection of the Cleveland State University Libraries)*

CLEVELAND'S DOWNTOWN DEPARTMENT STORES

WILLIAM TAYLOR AND SONS
FOUNDED ———————————— 1870
ORIGINAL LOCATION ———————— Public Square
ORIGINAL NAME ———————— Taylor, Kilpatrick & Company
FINAL LOCATION ———————— Euclid & East Sixth
DATE CLOSED ———————— December 16, 1961

THE BAILEY COMPANY
FOUNDED ———————————— 1881
ORIGINAL LOCATION ———————— Prospect & East Second
ORIGINAL NAME ———————— Lewis A. Bailey Company
FINAL LOCATION ———————— Prospect & Ontario
DATE CLOSED ———————— March 22, 1962

STERLING LINDER
FOUNDED ———————————— 1874
ORIGINAL LOCATION ———————— Warehouse District
ORIGINAL NAMES ———————— Beckwith Sterling & Co., Sterling & Welch, Sterling Lindner Davis

FINAL LOCATION ———————— Euclid & East 13th
DATE CLOSED ———————— September 21, 1968

THE HALLE BROTHERS COMPANY
FOUNDED ———————————— 1891
ORIGINAL LOCATION ———————— West Superior
ORIGINAL NAME ———————— Halle Brothers
FINAL LOCATION ———————— Euclid & East 12th
DATE CLOSED ———————— January 27, 1982

THE MAY COMPANY
FOUNDED ———————————— 1899
ORIGINAL LOCATION ———————— Ontario near Public Square
ORIGINAL NAME ———————— The May Company
FINAL LOCATION ———————— Public Square
DATE CLOSED ———————— January 31, 1992

DILLARD'S
FOUNDED ———————————— 1860
ORIGINAL LOCATION ———————— West Superior, near Public Square
ORIGINAL NAMES ———————— Hower & Higbee, The Higbee Company
CURRENT LOCATION ———————— Public Square

Mantis James (M.J.) Van Sweringen
(Shaker Historical Museum)

Oris Paxton (O.P.) Van Sweringen
(Shaker Historical Museum)

Once the avenue of stately homes and overhanging trees and nicknamed Millionaire's Row for the elegance of the mansions which lined it, by the turn of the century lower Euclid Avenue (west of Erie Street) had already experienced the same phenomenon that earlier had transformed Public Square. When the first homes were being built along Euclid Avenue, the location had seemed safely remote from the West Superior business district. By 1900, however, the lower avenue had become a shopping and office area, and the commercial district was rapidly expanding eastward along the upper avenue. In 1908 the opening of the large Hippodrome Theatre, next door to the new Taylor's store, helped solidify the role that entertainment would also play in the avenue's growing commercial mix. The Hippodrome joined the Euclid Avenue Opera House on East Fourth Street just south of Euclid (1875), and the Star Theatre (1887, formerly known as the Columbia and later as the Embassy) two doors east of East Sixth Street.

The affluent Clevelanders who had taken such pride in their homes along the famous avenue found the intrusion of vulgar business and the noise it generated too much to endure. They did not hesitate to sell their old home sites--for a tidy profit of course--and relocate themselves to the distant "heights" communities then under development in the eastern suburbs.

Onto the scene around this time stepped the Van Sweringen brothers, who in 1909 had optioned four acres of land adjacent to the southwest quadrant of Public Square as a location to build an interurban railway station. The two brothers, Oris Paxton (known as O.P.) and Mantis James (M.J.), also presented their center-city location as an alternative to the proposed lakefront railroad station facility. Clevelanders quickly took up sides, and conflict over the eventual choice of locations would provide fodder for over a decade of municipal debate.

The Van Sweringen brothers had been born in rural Wayne County, about 50 miles to the southwest of Cleveland, the sons of James T. (prophetically, for "Tower") and Jennie Curtis Sweringen. O.P. was born in 1879, his brother two years later; they were inseparable companions throughout their lives. Their family moved to Cleveland in 1891 and settled in a home on Doan Avenue (East 105th Street) near Cedar Avenue. The brothers earned their first pennies by delivering newspapers in the area of North Union Village (today's Shaker Heights). Established by followers of the Shaker religion, the community had shrunk to less than 30 residents by 1889, when it was dissolved. By the time the brothers came onto the scene, the lands formerly home to the North Union settlement were essentially abandoned. The diminishing numbers of the celibate sect had moved on to other Shaker communities in Ohio and New York. As the boys delivered papers, they did

The candy store at the southwest quadrant of the Square and Ontario street is where the Humphrey family got its start in business. In 1905 the family would take over Euclid Beach Park. It was also the future site for the Van Sweringens' Public Square development. *(Bruce Young Collection)*

so through largely open lands. The brothers later worked for the Bradley Chemical Company in the Society for Savings Building on Public Square. Their early work experiences familiarized the brothers with the two areas of Greater Cleveland that would later make their reputation and fortune.

The brothers turned their interests to real estate as they entered young adulthood. After a few successful transactions along Carnegie Avenue, they invested in some property in suburban Lakewood. There their ventures were unsuccessful, and their properties ended in foreclosure.

Determined to change their fortune, the brothers then changed their name back to the original "Van" Sweringen--the "Van" had been dropped earlier to seem more "American"-- and shifted their focus to the east side of town. They bought land in Cleveland Heights along North Park Boulevard and then Fairmount Boulevard. Realizing that the Fairmount development was too far from downtown to flourish without access to convenient public transportation, the Vans persuaded the Cleveland Railway Company to build what became the Fairmount Boulevard streetcar line. With convenient public access thus assured, the upscale properties along Fairmount found a ready market. Soon the Fairmount development thrived, a triumph for the brothers which secured their financial future. They were no longer poor men.

In 1905, the brothers took an option on the former Shaker land and bought the acreage for $1 million. In this new venture, they decided to plan an entire community, replete with strict zoning codes which required that every residence be distinctive. They laid out the community with broad boulevards (capable of handling streetcar tracks inside a grassy median strip),

The Van Sweringens had their first successes in real estate development in the Heights communities. Upscale properties such as this home they built for themselves and their sisters became their hallmark. *(Shaker Historical Museum)*

winding side thoroughfares, and with considerable acreage set aside for park land. They specified that no home be built for a cost less than $17,000 (an equivalent today of approximately $180,000).

They again realized that the success of their model community depended upon public transportation. Rebuffed by the Cleveland Railway Company in their attempts to get the company to build another streetcar line to run along Shaker Boulevard, the brothers eventually paid for the line's construction themselves. The new line branched off the Fairmount line car line, and then traveled south along Coventry Boulevard to Shaker Boulevard and then eastward through the development. The trip to and from downtown Cleveland via that route, however, was too circuitous to be truly appealing to residents, and this consideration prompted the brothers to decide they would build a direct "rapid transit" line to downtown. That, in turn, led to their option for property adjacent to the Square's southwest quadrant.

Believing that the natural ravine west of what would become Shaker Square would be ideal for their rail line, they approached the Nickel Plate Railroad for permission to cross that company's right-of-way. Nickel Plate Railroad officials, though, shocked the brothers with the price required for an easement. So in another bold stroke the Van Sweringens in 1916 bought the entire 513-mile Nickel Plate Railroad for $8.5 million.

This purchase launched the real estate developers into another business, one which in characteristic fashion they pursued avidly. Over the next decade the brothers would continue to buy railroad properties, until eventually they controlled nearly 27,000 miles of railroad right-of-way. They became the fourth largest railroad operators in the eastern United States. Essentially, this had come about in order to gain access to a mere five miles of trackage rights for their rapid transit line.

Construction on their Cleveland Interurban Railroad line (later renamed the Shaker Heights Rapid Transit and today the Shaker and Van Aken Lines of the Regional Transit Authority) began in 1916. But their plans for the station on the Square remained on hold. The city fathers were still holding out for the terminal to be built on the lakefront. It would take until the end of the decade for that issue to be settled.

As Cleveland's second decade of the century opened, the city had climbed one notch on the list of the United States' largest cities. In 1910 the U.S. Census Bureau reported that the nation's sixth city had a population of 560,663.

Cleveland in 1910 also found itself with a new mayor. Tom L. Johnson had served four terms as mayor, but in his last term he found himself outmaneuvered by the city's private streetcar interests. He was also facing failing health and a citizenry tired of the prolonged battle over

The Cleveland Union Terminal project underwent many conceptual changes between 1909 when it was first conceived and 1930 when it was completed. This sketch by the project's main architects reveals an early idea for the union station. *(Cleveland Union Terminal Archives of Cleveland State University Libraries)*

the city's streetcar lines which had resulted in considerable disruption of service. Physically and emotionally drained, Johnson was unable to campaign as vigorously as he had in the past, and he was defeated at the polls in November 1909. Herman Baehr succeeded him in office. Johnson did not long survive the defeat. His illness took his life on April 10, 1911.

Though rebuffed by the voters, Johnson's contributions were not forgotten. Plans were soon underway to honor him with a statue on Public Square. In 1914 workmen removed the fountain at the center of the northwest quadrant to make way for the Johnson monument.

Designed by Cleveland artist Herman Matzen, the monument consisted of a low platform surmounted by a bronze statue of the late mayor. He was depicted in a seated position, holding a book in his right hand, a depiction of *Progress and Poverty,* the volume which outlined the liberal ideals of Johnson's mentor, Henry George. Matzen explained that he wanted to "represent a thoroughly democratic character," and create a "monument for the people, one which would allow little children to mount it and climb into his [the mayor's] lap." It took nearly two years to complete work on the monument. Johnson's statue, cast by the Gorham Company of New York City, was finally settled onto its base at 10:23 a.m. on April 4, 1916, 15 years to the minute from the time that Johnson had taken his first oath of office as mayor of the Forest City. The statue faced southeast towards the Superior/ Ontario intersection. A small crowd of about 200 were present for the event. To further honor the liberal ideals of the mayor, behind the statue, near the West Roadway, a

The Tom L. Johnson monument was installed on the northeast quadrant of the Square in 1916. It was a fond tribute of the people to the dynamic leadership he provided the city in the first decade of the century. *(Greg Deegan photo)*

three-step rostrum was installed to provide Clevelanders with a forum for free speech. The northwest quadrant thus became Cleveland's version of London's Hyde Park corner. Over the next six decades (until the rostrum was removed in the 1980s revamping of the Square) evangelists, politicians, social activists, ordinary citizens, and assorted loonies as well, made ample use of the little free speech platform.

At the same time that the Johnson statue was dedicated, the northwest quadrant also received a small kiosk which housed a temperature gauge. The thermometer provided scientific measurement of the hot or cold extremes which Clevelanders walking across the open spaces of the Square could all too readily feel.

While the Van Sweringen development in the Heights was gaining new residents, Public Square was achieving some new heights of its own. Two more skyscrapers were built along its western half during the century's second decade. W. G. Marshall had begun his career working at the May Drug Store on the southwest corner of Public Square and Ontario Street. In 1912 he founded what would become the Marshall drug store chain and began construction on a new headquarters office building for his growing company. Located on the corner of the northwest quadrant of the Square and Superior Avenue and designed by Cleveland architect W. S. Lougee, the terra cotta building rose 13 stories. The Marshall Building (later One Public Square Building) was completed in 1913. Just after the new building opened, as a promotion a Cleveland Baseball Club employee would occasionally release specially marked balloons from the building's roof. Any person returning one of them would qualify for tickets to an upcoming Cleveland Naps baseball game at League Park.

The Marshall Building's gleaming terra cotta facade brightened the northwest quadrant of Public Square when it opened in 1913. To its right is the 1895 American Trust Building (originally named the Mohawk Building) *(Cleveland Picture Collection of Cleveland Public Library)*

The other major new office building on the perimeter of Public Square opened in 1915. The 15-story Cleveland Electric Illuminating Company Building (now called the 75 Public Square Building) was erected on the site of the old Wick Block and Lyceum Theater, between the Cuyahoga County Courthouse and the Old Stone Church. Designed by the prominent Cleveland architectural partnership of Hubbell and Benes, the narrow brick-and-terra-cotta-faced building was the home of the utility until 1958 when it moved into its new building next door at 55 Public Square.

With the departure of competitors William Taylor Sons and Company and Sterling and Welch to upper Euclid Avenue, the May Company, under the leadership of Nathan L. Dauby, head of the local May's operation, seized the opportunity to take a giant leap forward on its promise to Clevelanders to "Watch us Grow." In 1905 May's had purchased two buildings that faced Prospect Avenue, and in 1906 it was able to secure title to Taylor's former home in the old Cushing Block facing on Public Square. The first steps in securing a site for a new building had been taken.

As May's was buying property, its Bailey Company neighbor was already building. In 1907 it put up a ten-story annex on Ontario Street, immediately north of its main building. It then had the distinction of being Public Square's largest department store—but not for long.

In 1907, May's also got going on construction. To increase its existing merchandising space while construction would be underway on a new Public Square building, May's added two more stories to its original store on Ontario Street and erected a four-story annex to its north. With the added space in its Ontario buildings, the May Company was free to raze its Public Square annex to prepare the site for the new main store building. By 1912 May's controlled all the property it needed, and work began on clearing of the site east of Farnham Alley, stretching from Prospect Avenue to Public Square.

In 1915 the May Company opened its large new department store building on Public Square. In 1931 the structure would grow even larger when two more floors were added. *(Cleveland Press Collection of the Cleveland State University Libraries)*

The new building, designed by Daniel Burnham and Company of Chicago, was a giant. Rising six stories with white terra cotta frontages on both Public Square and Prospect sides, the new building gave the May Company one million square feet of new space, which the company said could conveniently accommodate 150,000 shoppers at a time. The gleaming emporium was state of the art in terms of commercial design. Awnings stretched across the Public Square frontage, affording window shoppers some shelter from the elements, and two recessed entranceways provided additional window display area. Inside patrons appreciated even more the 23 elevators and four sets of moving stairways. The escalators, with grooved wood treds, significantly eased traveling between selling floors. They were the first in Cleveland. The new building also offered a children's playroom and an auditorium for lectures and musical entertainments. It was the nation's most modern department store and the largest in Ohio.

The May Company officially opened its new building on Monday, October 18, 1915, with a week-long sale. It offered an assortment of fashion specials for women: that week ladies' suits were selling for $19.75, regular $10.00 hats for $4.95, and red fox sets for $75.00. Double Eagle stamps were an added bonus for Tuesday shoppers. Bailey's countered with a sale "event unequaled in value-giving in Cleveland retail store history." Its women's suits were priced at $19.50, its regular silk and velvet $5.00 hats were $1.00, and its red fox sets were only $47.50. Bailey's also offered double stamps on Tuesday; they used Merchants' red stamps.

Bailey's had better prices, but the May's store got the larger crowds.

The city was not only engaged in commercial expansion, it was still working on completing the Group Plan. In 1914 Cleveland Mayor Newton D. Baker unveiled plans for the Group Plan railroad station facing Lakeside Avenue at the northern edge of the Mall. Blueprints showed the lakefront station occupying a 53-acre site that would require considerable additional lakefront filling. Designed by the Chicago firm of Burnham & Company, the station itself would rise six stories, its neo-classical facade covered in granite and marble, and its front portico lined with pillars three stories tall. Pedestrians would enter the station through the street-level portico, but those arriving by streetcar would be whisked by a short subway directly to the station's lower ticketing area. Ramps would carry passengers from the station's waiting room to the track level below. The plans were warmly welcomed by many since the old station had become increasingly less hospitable to patrons. An ongoing repair job to the old depot had left patrons boarding or alighting from trains without any cover from the elements. Bakker's announcement, of course, was not synonymous with the start of construction. Explaining the renovation of the

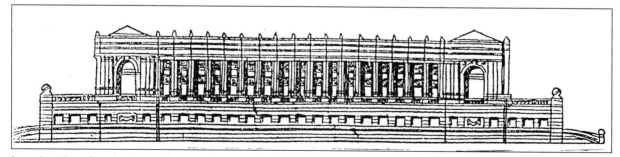

In a battle of public relations releases, in 1915 the city published this preliminary sketch of the proposed lakefront railroad station. In this view from the Mall only the upper stories of the edifice are shown. Three more floors were below Mall level. The concept was drawn by the Graham, Burnham Company of Chicago. (Cleveland Press *collection of the Cleveland State University Libraries*)

73-year-old station, railroad spokesman D. C. Moon explained, "You councilman may be grayhaired before you see the new union depot." Moon clearly recognized that before any construction could begin, myriad details and agreements between the railroads and the city would still have to be negotiated.

The engineering studies being carried out for the Group Plan station on the lakefront did not deter the Van Sweringen brothers. Their engineers were also busy at the drafting tables, and the

The ongoing debate about the location for the new railroad station kept the Van Sweringens' plans on hold, and kept the southwest quadrant of Public Square in its dingy dress. Ontario Street is to the left. *(Bruce Young Collection)*

brothers had increased their holdings south of the Square. In 1915 the Ohio legislature authorized operation of joint electric interurban and steam railroad stations. Eagerly sought by the brothers, this provision paved the way for a dual-purpose station at Public Square, an advantage that proponents of the lakefront station could not claim. The new legislation kept the Vans' expanding dreams for Public Square moving forward.

On the other hand, the city of Cleveland could not support two new union railroad facilities, and the Group Plan station on the lakefront remained the preferred option of city officials. That plan received the official go ahead in August 1915, when Cleveland City Council approved a contract with several of the railroad companies to move ahead with the union station there. Not all railroad companies, however, had signed the lakefront agreement. The main dissenters did not enter downtown via the lakeshore trackage, but from the south. The Van Sweringen brothers began to court the railroads which would not benefit from a lakeshore station, and that consideration certainly contributed to their deciding in 1916 to take over the Nickel Plate Railroad.

The Vans and the city fathers were thus moving along different tracks. Eventually, though, the parties would find themselves on a collision course. One party would have to get out of the way.

While plans for the Public Square station were thus temporarily stymied, the Van Sweringen brothers remained confident their plan would ultimately prevail. They reckoned that a new hotel would nicely complement their planned railroad and interurban station, and in the meantime it would also serve as an indicator to the public of just how comprehensively the Van Sweringen plans would redevelop the properties southwest of the city green. That southwest section had been untouched by 20th century improvements, and the faded and sooty buildings there were increasingly out of place with their taller, newer, and better designed neighbors facing the other quadrants.

On April 11, 1916, a Van Sweringens' spokesman announced their plans to build a new hotel on the site of the old Forest City House along the southwest quadrant of the Square. The hotel project, as it was then described, was to be a part of a $50 million undertaking that would later include an office building and the proposed union station. Later that spring the Vans' Cleveland Hotel Company purchased the property, and on September 16, 1916, after 64 years of service to the traveling public, the begrimed Forest City House

In 1918 the impressive Hotel Cleveland opened for business. It was the first phase in the Van Sweringens' plans for their Public Square station complex. Across Superior Avenue from it is the Marshall Building. *(Bruce Young Collection)*

bade farewell to its last guest and closed its doors for the last time. Demolition began shortly thereafter.

The brothers hired the Chicago firm of Graham, Burnham & Company (successor to the Daniel Burnham and Company firm) to design the replacement. The new hotel would be a giant, boasting 1,000 rooms (hotel rooms in those days were very small by modern standards, but the train traveler of the era deemed them more than satisfactory). In order to provide each of the guest rooms with a window, an important feature in the days before the advent of central air conditioning, the frontage along Superior avenue took the shape of a letter "E." The hotel had two entrances, one facing Public Square, the other Superior Avenue. Rising 14 stories, the light grey granite and brick-faced building brought a bright and imposing new presence to the Square. The hotel opened to the public on December 16, 1918. The building reassured Clevelanders that even the restrictions and the uncertainties of the Great War years had not slowed their city's steady march toward greatness.

Even as the hotel was underway, however, talk continued about building the railway station on the lakefront. Voters had approved bonds for Public Auditorium in April 1916, but at the time the city was not certain where to locate the new convention facility. One plan called for it to be located on the west side of the Mall, between Lakeside and St. Clair avenues. Another choice would put it on the east side of the Mall at East Sixth Street. A third site, however, also had its advocates, and it was strongly supported by the Cleveland *Press*. This plan would have put the new hall right on the lakefront, immediately north of the original Group Plan union depot site. Advocates pointed out that the proximity of the Public Auditorium to the railroad station would prove to be a major plus to out-of-town convention planners.

Another plan for Public Square was also in the works. By 1919 the Cleveland Railway Company's streetcars were operating at saturation levels. In order to carry the crush loads of passengers, the Railway had adopted the expedient of attaching non-motor trailers to its streetcars, thus doubling the capacity of each unit. Still, headways were very close together, and only so many streetcars each hour could navigate the Public Square loops. To increase capacity, the city proposed building short subways with five turning loops and passenger waiting stations beneath Public Square.

The advantages of subway running had made been made clear to Clevelanders on December 25, 1918, when the first revenue service streetcars took advantage of their exclusive right-of-way on the lower deck of the new Detroit-Superior Bridge to speed their way from West 25th Street to West Sixth Street and Superior Avenue, unimpeded by other traffic. The new subway plan, by the New York consulting firm of Barclay, Parsons & Klapp, would have extended the bridge subway beneath Superior Avenue to Public Square. Streetcars arriving from the east via Euclid Avenue would enter a subway at East 22nd Street. Those coming in via St. Clair, Superior, or

By 1915 streetcar traffic was on the increase, cars frequenty bunched together, as this scene on Superior Avenue and Public Square shows. To ease the problem, the Detroit - Superior Bridge was under construction to the west, and city planners were beginning to think about building a downtown subway. *(Bruce Young Collection)*

Payne avenues would begin subway running at East Ninth Street and Superior Avenue, and those arriving from the southeast would begin the descent to subway trackage at Ontario Street and Eagle Avenue (about where the Gateway plaza is presently located). The plan would require a $15 million bond issue to be approved by city voters. It would also necessitate extensive excavation on Public Square.

While more dramatic changes in the form of the new union station and the Public Square subway station were waiting in the wings, the completion of Hotel Cleveland brought to a close the actual physical changes to the Public Square environs during the first two decades of the century. The citizens of Cleveland would soon determine whether the station and subway plans would get underway in the next decade.

The story of Public Square at the start of the 20th century is, of course, not limited to the construction activity that took place there. The center-city green continued during the first two decades of the century as the focal point for the rituals of community and civic life. As had been true in the past, the events that were conducted in Public Square were as varied as they were numerous.

In September 1901 Public Square was festooned in white pylons and ribbons to welcome to Cleveland the annual encampment of the Grand Army of the Republic, the national association

The U.S. flag is at half mast and the pylons in the Square marking the encampment of the Grand Army of the Republic have been ribboned in black. The Square is paying tribute to slain U.S. President William McKinley. *(Cleveland Picture Collection of Cleveland Public Library)*

of Union Army Civil War veterans.   The Soldiers and Sailors monument was to be the focal point of the ceremonies, and native son and then-President William McKinley, himself a Union Army veteran, was to address the assembly.   He was scheduled to arrive in Cleveland on September 7, but the day before in Buffalo, New York, McKinley was mortally wounded by an assassin's bullet.   Overnight, the Square's formerly festive appearance was transformed to a more somber one as attendants entwined black ribbons with the white in a show of solidarity with the fallen leader.   The encampment activities continued, but on a markedly less celebratory note as McKinley clung to life.   He lost that battle on September 14.   Some Clevelanders suggested that a fountain in McKinley's memory be built on the northwest quadrant of the Square, but nothing came of that idea.

Public Square had become the place where the citizens of Cleveland memorialized their leaders.   On July 1, 1905, Clevelander and U. S. Secretary of State John Hay died.   His memorial services were held in the Chamber of Commerce Building with crowds lining up in the Square to pay their last respects.   Former mayor Tom L. Johnson died in Cleveland on April 10,

World War I still raged in Europe on Flag Day in 1918, making the ceremony on the southeast quadrant of the Square that day more poignant for observers. Behind the flag are the Marshall Building (left) and the Ulmer Building (right). *(Cleveland* Press *Collection of the Cleveland State University Libraries)*

1911. Rather than be buried in his adopted city, he had made it known that he wished his interment to be in Brooklyn, New York, in the same cemetery where his mentor, Henry George, lay. Police estimated that 200,000 Clevelanders came downtown to bid farewell to the populist leader. They filled Public Square and lined the entire route from the Square to the Union Depot at the foot of West Ninth Street and watched in silence as the cortege bore Johnson's coffin to trackside.

When the Great War broke out in Europe in 1914, Clevelanders were more concerned with their nation's then ongoing conflicts in the Caribbean and with Mexico. These events seemed closer at hand. But as the European war deepened, the U.S. government decided that it could not sustain its original intentions of neutrality. On April 6, 1917, the country declared war on the Central Powers. With its large ethnic population of Germans and Hungarians, Cleveland clearly was divided over the wisdom of the declaration of war. Despite the tensions that ethnic differences made palpable, in general the city was unified in its public support of the nation's war effort. Clevelanders took pride in the fact that their former mayor, Newton D. Baker, was President Woodrow Wilson's secretary of war, and furthermore, most Clevelanders were benefiting from the boom in the local economy brought about by wartime manufacturing demands.

On the 11th day of the 11th month, but somewhat after the 11th hour of 1918, revelers line Superior Avenue as they celebrate the armistice that ended the Great War. In the background is the Federal Building. *(Cleveland* Press *Collection of the Cleveland State University Libraries)*

A focal point in the local support of the war effort was a series of rallies which supported the U.S. government Liberty Loan bond program. Clevelanders set a per capita record with the first bond drive in June 1917, and they rallied again in Public Square later that same month to subscribe to the local Red Cross's war relief fund. Clevelanders again massed in Public Square on October 1, 1917, when popular Cleveland Indians outfielder Tris Speaker keyed the city's second bond rally. Once again Clevelanders oversubscribed to the bond sale. Clevelanders proudly did the same in two more bond drives in 1918, and with only mild grumbling they put up with the many restrictions which the wartime economy had imposed.

When word reached the city on November 11, 1918, that an armistice had been signed, the Greater Cleveland community rightly felt that their patriotic support on the job, in their sacrifices, and in their bond purchases had played a genuine role in the Allied triumph. Cleveland Mayor Harry L. Davis declared a holiday, and hundreds of thousands of Greater Cleveland citizens converged on Public Square and the downtown area to celebrate. Throughout the day and well into the night, Clevelanders attended church services, sang patriotic songs, marched, and shot off fireworks.

The postwar years would bring new achievements and even more triumphs to the proud city, and at the city's heart in both its architectural profile and its civic role, Public Square would come to shine ever more brightly.

Boom, Bust, and War
1920 - 1949

It was the people's trek to the ballot box that ultimately decided what would happen to Public Square during the 1920s and into the future. Transportation issues were key to two important city-wide votes. One, in 1920, concerned the proposed subway that would utilize the town green as the hub of Cleveland's streetcar lines, and the other, in 1919, was designed to settle the question of where to put the long-debated new union station.

On January 7, 1919, area residents awoke to the news on the front page of *The Plain Dealer*: "Union Station Carries 3 to 2." Although a nondescript headline concerning a local ordinance in a special election, the news heralded what would become the greatest alteration to Cleveland's Public Square. The town's civic center had welcomed several new buildings encapsulating its area in the previous decade, but the issue taken to voters proposed to make the central green even more the city's hub.

Streetcars and one horse-drawn carriage maneuver through the Square. The automobile was still not dominant as the 1920s began. In the background, the land adjacent to the southwest quadrant has been cleared to make way for the construction of the union terminal. *(Bruce Young Collection)*

While the 1919 vote promised to remake the perimeter of the Square, the 1920 vote would have resulted in changes to Public Square itself. Voters, however, balked. There would be no subway. Part of the reason these issues had become urgent was Cleveland's continuing population growth.

Between 1910 and 1920, Cleveland's boom had continued, the population rising 42 % over the 1910 census figures to 796,841 people. Downtown Cleveland was not only northern Ohio's business and financial center, it was also the region's shopping hub. The May Company at Public Square, the Bailey Company just south on Prospect Avenue and Ontario Street, and Euclid Avenue stores such as William Taylor and Sons, the Higbee Company, and Halle Brothers Company made downtown a shopping mecca. In addition, by 1922 a completed Playhouse Square on Euclid Avenue between East 14th and East 17th streets invited Clevelanders downtown to enjoy the theater. A steady stream of people, both night and day, managed their way through the bustling metropolis.

Because of the congestion that this growth entailed, city council had proposed to the voters that something be done to ameliorate the deteriorating downtown traffic situation. Problems in negotiating the busy downtown streets stemmed partly from near-capacity operation of the streetcar system and partly from the growing popularity of the automobile. As the autos and

Cleveland utilized combination motor/trailer streetcar trains in order to ease downtown traffic congestion. Had the subway been approved, crowds, such as these awaiting to board in Public Square and obstructing traffic, would have been a thing of the past. *(Cleveland Railway photo, Blaine Hays Collection)*

streetcars competed for more road space, traffic difficulties multiplied. That reality was what prompted City Council to endorse a plan by the Barclay, Parsons & Klapp consulting firm that would have created five streetcar loops beneath Public Square with the trolleys reaching them by means of short downtown subways. Despite Cleveland Railway Company's reluctance to buy into the plan, since it would increase the company's operating costs, City Council in April 1920 took the proposal to the voters, hoping for their approval of a $15 million bond issue to finance the subway. After much public debate, voters rejected the bond issue handily, 30,017 to 13,099. City voters were not so much rejecting the idea of a subway as they were the method for its financing. Clevelanders felt that the financial obligation should be shared by suburbanites.

Though the issue was defeated, the traffic problems remained, and so the idea of a subway, with Public Square as the hub, did not die with the 1920 vote. One idea was the "penny subway" proposal put forth in 1925. The suggestion was for Cleveland Railway to raise its fares by a penny, so that the extra money could be put into a subway trust fund. Another proposal by a local real estate leader suggested a subway line from Public Square to University Circle under Chester Avenue. A year later, City Manager William R. Hopkins recommended a line between the same two points--Public Square and University Circle--under Euclid Avenue. And again, a decade later, city officials entertained other proposals of underground railways that would loop under the town center, much like the 1920 proposal.

Ultimately, though, while the various plans were the subjects of community forums and local media attention, none of these later ideas advanced beyond the proposal stage. During the 1920s city council members found themselves having to weigh priorities: spending money to facilitate the booming new housing industry or providing outlays for more efficient public transportation systems. By 1930, the city's need to keep pace with the activity of the home construction industry and the worsening economic conditions brought about by the Depression served to postpone serious consideration of these other transportation plans.

As for the union terminal, the voters of Cleveland settled that long-festering dispute on January 6, 1919. More than 30,000 voters favored the Van Sweringen plan over the lakefront one (30,758 to 19,916), paving the way for a vast project that would change the city's green in a dramatic way.

The construction site for the union terminal in 1925 is overshadowed by the Hotel Cleveland. In the foreground, one of Cleveland's short-lived double-decker buses heads west. The pagoda on the northeast quadrant also served as a visitor information center. *(Cleveland Railway photo, Blaine Hays Collection)*

Cleveland was entering upon perhaps its most prosperous and successful decade in the 20th century when in 1920 work began on the union terminal project. The results of the voters' decision to locate the railroad station on the Van Sweringen property off the southwest quadrant of Public Square soon became visible. The work began with the clearing of 37 acres of downtown land as well as along a 17-mile corridor stretching from Collinwood to Linndale that would serve as an electrified right-of-way to the new station.

The downtown complex envisioned by the Van Sweringens was far more than just a joint interurban/railroad passenger station. The recently completed Hotel Cleveland was actually the first building of the project. Other structures in the grand plan were to include a new main post office facility on Huron Road, a department store, and seven office buildings, one located on the Square, between the hotel and department store, and the others situated between Prospect Avenue and Huron Road.

One of the early conceptual designs for the union terminal complex called for changes on the southwest quadrant in which pedestrians would have direct access to the railway concourses. This idea gave way to the soaring Tower that would soon emerge on the Square. *(Western Reserve Historical Society)*

It was to be the office building on Public Square, however, that became the project's centerpiece and which would become the city's most famous landmark. Architectural work on what would become known as the Terminal Tower and most of the other buildings in the Terminal complex was done by Graham, Anderson, Probst & White, a nationally noted firm with main offices in Chicago (the new U.S. Post Office Building, however, was designed by the Cleveland firm of Walker and Weeks). The official groundbreaking for the Terminal Tower occurred on a rainy September 28, 1923. The Cleveland firm of John Gill and Sons was the general contractor for the project.

When the Van Sweringens first announced the Terminal project, they had planned to construct a central office building that would be relatively squat in structure. Rising some 14 stories above the station, it was to be surmounted by a cupola-style central core of about five additional floors. Before construction began, though, the plan was changed to add another 38 stories above the 14-story base. The Vans could foresee the attractiveness of office space at the new location and decided to build accordingly. The soaring Terminal Tower was the result. It bears a strong resemblance to the earlier New York Municipal Building, a product of McKim, White, and Meade, which suggests that Graham, Anderson, Probst & White made liberal use of plans available in their company's archives. Rather than commenting on that similarity, however, contemporary newspaper reports explained that the developers had altered the squat tower design because it resembled too closely a German helmet. The ravages of World War I were still fresh in the collective consciousness, and anti-German sentiment was still prevalent.

By 1927 the future look of the Square was already becoming apparent. Steel work on the Terminal Tower is at the halfway point. *(Cleveland Union Terminal Archives of the Cleveland State University Libraries)*

The Tower project pioneered a significant new concept in construction: the use of "air rights." Air rights involve erecting one building above the property of another, in this case the Tower over the station. The Terminal's "basement" was actually part of the Union Terminal's concourse area. Also built on air rights over the track level were the U.S. Post Office Building as well as the three interconnected Prospect Buildings: the Midland, Medical Arts, and Builders Exchange buildings (today known as the Midland, LTV, and Guildhall buildings of the composite Cleveland Landmarks Towers.) The office buildings and the post office were connected to the union terminal by underground passageways.

While the Tower may not have had a true basement, it certainly had a solid foundation, with caissons dug nearly 200 feet deep to bedrock level. Workers had to dig through many layers of clay (some of it wet—giving rise to the often repeated statement that the Tower was built on top of "quicksand") to reach bedrock. Each pit was hand dug, and as workers loosened the clay, they put it into large buckets which were hoisted by cable to the surface. The pits were then filled with concrete.

Work on the Tower's structural steel skeleton began in September 1926, and took less than a year to complete. When construction crews lifted the last piece of steel into place on August 27, 1927, the Terminal Tower pierced the sky at 708 feet (not counting the 65-foot flagpole), a measurement taken from the concourse level of the union station. The Tower was the second tallest building in the U.S., behind only New York City's Woolworth Building, which was 792 feet tall. It was also the tallest building in the United States outside New York City. It held onto that latter distinction for 40 years, until laborers completed construction on Chicago's John Hancock Building in 1967. The Tower cost $65 million.

In early 1927 the Terminal Tower is more than half complete, but the parts of the development that would rise south of Prospect Avenue have not yet begun. *(Bruce Young Collection)*

When Cleveland Union Terminal opened, it gave the Van Sweringens' Shaker Heights rapid transit trains direct access to Public Square. Here a five-car train is posed at the entrance to the traction concourse. *(E.W. Jenny photo, Jim Toman Collection)*

The complex's distinction was not limited to just the Tower, however. The project's raison d'etre, after all, was as a railroad and interurban station. The station area consisted of three concourses, two flanking traction concourses to serve the interurban electric railways, and a central steam ticket lobby and skylighted concourse for the mainline railroads. Situated throughout the station level were various shops and restaurants. Below the concourses was track level, which had the capacity of handling a total of 34 tracks, 24 for the railroads and 10 for the rapid transit, although in fact only three were actually put into use for traction and another 10 for the mainline railroads. The steam concourse was called the largest waiting room in the world without interior pillars for support. The first train to use the new facility was May 19, 1930, and the Vans' Cleveland Interurban Rapid Transit line from Shaker Heights made its first trip into the station on July 20.

The grand opening for Cleveland Union Terminal took place on June 28, 1930, and drew the attention of the nation. *The Plain Dealer* accounts tell of the impact the new complex had on Clevelanders and on the world. Referring to it as the "Vans' Taj Majal," writers lauded the brothers' civic vision, also calling the Union Terminal complex the "Pinnacle of Civic Greatness." Some observers noted that the development rejuvenated Public Square and made the Sixth City the gateway of continental travel as well as the center of the city's railway transit system. The entire project was built at a cost of $179 million ($2.71 billion in 1998 figures).

With all the hype that surrounded the complex's completion, it was no surprise that on the day of the Union Terminal's grand opening an estimated 40,000 people came to the complex throughout the day. Although the doors were slated to open at 10:00 a.m., throngs of people started to

The newly completed Terminal Tower dominates the Square in 1930. To the left of the Tower, the Higbee store is under construction, soon to complete the Van Sweringen's complex. *(Blaine Hays Collection)*

gather at 6:30 a.m., curious to witness the sparkling new facility. They strolled down the four ramps leading from the Public Square portico to the three gleaming marble-walled concourses below. There they could gaze through the bronze-framed display windows of the various boutiques. They could check the arrival and departure display board, and no doubt their ears were tuned to the train announcer's boarding and arrival calls and to the faint rumble of arriving and departing trains at track level below.

Of the people that attended the grand opening, 3,000 had been invited to partake in festivities celebrating the occasion. Guides first toured the invited guests and dignitaries through the new structure. Then, the New York Central and the Cleveland Grays bands played for the guests and crowd, and after a luncheon for those invited, speeches were delivered by notable figures. Henry Jouett, the chief engineer of the project; Julius H. Barnes, the chairman of the board of the U.S. Chamber of Commerce; and Patrick E. Crowley, the president of the New York Central Railroad, were among those who addressed the assembled dignitaries. They lauded the progress of the city and the civic vision of the Van Sweringen brothers. Conspicuously absent from the day's activities, however, were the reclusive O.P. and M.J. Van Sweringen.

Invited guests at the grand opening of Cleveland Union Terminal on June 28, 1930, enjoy a luncheon on the steam concourse. The reclusive Van Sweringen brothers were not among the assembled dignitaries for the event. *(Cleveland* Press *Collection of the Cleveland State University Libraries)*

Those present saw the complex as an act of bold defiance hurled against the threatening forces of economic downturn and as the promise of an approaching nationwide recovery. Organizers encouraged guests to take in the sights of the steam and traction concourses and to take a free ride on the clean and quiet electric trains running below.

The day and the complex united Cleveland in many ways. Its opening was a celebration of architectural grandeur and a new symbol of America's Sixth City.

The dreams of using the station as a hub for the interurban trolley hub did not materialize, however. By the time the station opened, only two interurban lines--besides the Van's rapid transit to Shaker Heights--remained, and those were in decline. While not capturing all the potential that had been foreseen for the complex, the Cleveland Union Terminal development nonetheless changed the face of Public Square and brought renewed activity to the town's green.

The part of the complex that most caught Clevelanders's attention, however, was the Terminal Tower. The building rose 52 stories above the ground, with two 14-story arms angling away from the center and embracing the outer perimeter of the Square's southwest quadrant. On the southern side of the Tower, two additional wings, also 14 stories in height, extended from the central shaft of the Tower to Prospect Avenue. The central tower, 98 square feet, rose through the 34th floor. At the 31st to the 33rd floors, four pillars broke the smooth lines that marked the lower stories. At the 34th floor, the Tower narrowed, but retained its basic shape. At

The ornamental treatment of the Terminal Tower increases as the Tower stretches closer to the skies. This photo of the 32nd to the 42nd floors shows some of that detail. *(Cleveland* Press *Collection of the Cleveland State University Libraries)*

the 37th floor, the Tower became cylindrical in shape. Additional pillars adorned the 41st to the 43rd floors, and at the 44th floor, the building narrowed again until the 52nd story, at which the Tower's shape became conical. From the 44th floor and above, the design was largely ornamental, as the floor space was much too small for any practical purpose. Elevator service ended at the 42nd floor, and following two more flights of stairs, the space from the 44th to the 52nd floor was served by a spiral metal staircase.

The design of the Tower provided the city with an instant and enduring architectural landmark. Subsequent skyscrapers of the modernist style built into the 1980s were more boxlike in design, largely devoid of ornamentation. Although many taller structures now grace the

When the Terminal Tower complex was completed in 1934 (the Post Office Building at the lower left was the last building to be constructed), the city's skyline was radically transformed. In the center foreground is the structure which held the skylight for the Union Terminal's steam concourse. *(Robert Runyon photo, Bruce Young Collection)*

skylines of major cities all over the nation, few have had the visual impact that Cleveland's landmark possessed, or, for that matter, continues to exude even today. Its setbacks and the changing shape in its upper stories make the Terminal Tower seem even taller than it actually is, giving the building a soaring image. It has been this image which became the city's most familiar landmark and the Square's most impressive addition.

At ground level, the complex's main entranceway, which fronts Public Square, seemed almost as impressive to observers as did the Tower. The facade at the town green featured seven large arches, flanked by Ionic-styled columns. Each of the arches measured 18 feet across and 35 feet high, below which were the main doorways to the building. Above each door expanses of glass filled the archway. The five center archways led directly into the portico, from which two ramps led to the steam concourse. The two outer archways led to ramps that entered the two traction courses on the station level.

The portico, a 153-foot long hall, included passageways not only to the Station, but also to the Hotel Cleveland. An additional entrance was created when the Higbee Company department store opened its doors adjacent to the station and Tower in September 1931. The portico's floor was of Tennessee marble and its walls of Botticino marble. The portico rose 47 feet to its vaulted ceiling of precast ornamental plaster. Murals by the artist Jules Guerin graced the upper portions of the portico. They depicted commerce, industry, transportation, and the four elements: water, fire, air, and earth.

When the Union Terminal was new, train travel still dominated inter-city transportation. The steam concourse of the Cleveland Union Terminal remained a bustling place through the end of World War II, when other modes of transportation became favored. *Cleveland Press Collection of the Cleveland State University Libraries)*

Among the most popular features of the new complex was the observation deck on the tower's 42nd floor. First opened to visitors in 1928, before the rest of the structure had been completed, the observation deck drew more than 50,000 visitors during its first year.

Even though the Van Sweringens were able to impress many contemporary onlookers with the project's grandeur and beauty, their later fortunes would never match the legacy they left behind. When the stock market crash in 1929 initiated economic problems, the brothers' vast business empire was worth an estimated $4 billion (approximately $38 billion in contemporary dollars). Despite tightening credit, the brothers' optimism was not dulled, and they purchased the Missouri Pacific Railroad in 1930. The Depression grew deeper, though, and revenue from their many enterprises began to shrink, while their debt obligations remained. In 1934 these amounted to $73 million ($912 million today), and they could not meet the payments due. Coming to the brothers' rescue were two long-time friends, George A. Ball and George A. Tomlinson, principals in the Mid-America Corporation. The pair bought the Vans' assets for about $3.1 million, certainly one of the great bargains in history. The Vans were then brought into the new corporation in key management positions.

For a brief period, it seemed that O.P. and M.J. had weathered the worst, but the severe pressures they faced had taken a toll. M.J., the younger brother, suffered from high blood pressure. A bout with influenza proved one challenge more than he could handle, and he died in Lakeside Hospital on December 13, 1935. O.P. survived his brother's passing, but to observers, the fire seemed to diminish after his brother's death. On November 23, 1936, aboard a private railway car on his way to New York City, O.P. died during his sleep, the victim of a heart attack. He had survived his brother by less than a year.

In keeping with the monumental changes occurring on the perimeter of the Square, the city fathers decided that the Square itself needed to be updated. The last change had taken place with the installation of the Tom L. Johnson statue in 1916, and since that time the Square's quadrants had generally been neglected. In particular, the southwest quadrant's pond and bridge had become an eyesore to many Clevelanders. As one councilman complained, Public Square had become an "architectural monstrosity." Nothing happened immediately in the wake of his criticism, although some ideas did come forward. One would have elevated Ontario Street inside the Square onto a bridge arching over Superior Avenue. Another would have changed the Square into a traffic circle, but the idea of the city's green as a "Public Circle" did not achieve popular acclaim. These particular plans mercifully expired. Nonetheless, consensus had been achieved that to complement the new terminal, the Square needed a facelift as well.

The reconstruction was slated to be completed in time for the dedication of the Terminal Tower complex. The City began the work in March 1930, and within a few months had finished. Because the County was responsible for the maintenance of the southeast quadrant and the Soldiers and Sailors monument, that portion of the town green was unaltered by the renovations. Elsewhere on the Square, however, many changes modified the look of the city's hub. In the northeast quadrant, workers tore down the stone bandstand at its eastern edge and replaced it with a new fountain in the center of the quadrant. For both northern quadrants, new trees, shrubs and flowers were planted. New diagonal walkways crisscrossed each green.

The southwest quadrant witnessed the most dramatic physical transformation. Workers removed the comfort station (the public restroom), flattened the undulating lawn, filled in the lagoon, and removed the bridge that had once straddled it. They then moved the Moses

In February 1930 the Square's four quadrants were being renovated. The northeast quadrant reveals new plantings while still retaining the old placement of the reviewing stand. In the lower center, the Moses Cleaveland statue can still be seen near the corner of the southwest quadrant. (Cleveland Press *photo, Blaine Hays Collection*)

In 1930, the quadrants on the Square received a makeover. But what would become the Square's adjacent green—the Mall—was still only partially completed, the rest serving as a parking lot. Behind the Society for Savings Building is the Brotherhood of Locomotive Engineers Building. *(Jim Toman Collection)*

During the union station construction period, the roadway off the southwest quadrant was also redone. The road work would allow for streetcars to navigate the Square in clockwise fashion. *(Cleveland Union Terminal Archives of the Cleveland State University Libraries)*

Cleaveland statue from its resting place at the northeast corner of the quadrant to a more prominent position at the center. As with the other quadrants, they completed the job with new trees, shrubs, flowers, and diagonal walkways. What did escape the bulldozer, though, were the "pagoda" waiting stations.

While the subway proposals of the early 1920s lived only ephemerally, City leaders recognized that traffic congestion in the Public Square vicinity had worsened along with related safety problems for downtown commuters. They tried to alleviate traffic problems there without spending significant money. In response, Cleveland Railway in 1931 reversed the two southern streetcar loops in Public Square. Except around the northeast quadrant, streetcars had looped through the Square in a counterclockwise manner, jeopardizing passengers' safety by requiring them to board on the traffic side. Reversing the loops created much safer boarding conditions for streetcar riders. Reversal of the northwest quadrant loop did not take place until 1939. The changes were welcomed by riders and motorists alike.

The importance of the Terminal Tower was underscored when the Cleveland Chamber of Commerce agreed to become the building's first tenant in 1928, abandoning its long-time headquarters at 167 Public Square, just east of the Society for Savings Building. Its old home did not remain vacant very long, however, for it soon became the home of Cleveland College. The college, founded in 1925, was established to serve the continuing education needs of area adults. Just a year later, the fledgling institution gained a measure of permanence and prestige when Western Reserve University officially incorporated it as one of its undergraduate schools. In only four years, registration jumped from 1,500 to 6,000, which made its original home at East 20th and Euclid--in rented space above an automobile dealership--untenable. The college moved into the Chamber of Commerce Building in time for the 1929-1930 academic year. A large "Cleveland College" sign appeared above the first floor entrance, and it remained a familiar feature of the Square until 1953.

On the other side of the Square, another edifice did not fare as fortunately. The old Cuyahoga County Court House, made redundant by the opening of the new courthouse on Lakeside Avenue in 1911, met its fate at the hands of a demolition squad. The old court house, which had occupied land just northwest of the green on Frankfort Avenue, was razed in 1935 to make room for more parking space--a sure sign of the times and of the popularity of the automobile.

Parking lots, of course, did not bring people to Public Square. Commercial attractions did. The Higbee Company, a Cleveland original since 1860, drew to the Square perhaps the most area residents ever when it opened the doors of its new flagship store in the Terminal Tower complex on September 8, 1931.

Even when the buildings around the Square did not change, their uses often did. In 1929 Cleveland College moved in to the old Chamber of Commerce building. The school served as a link between downtown's two central greens. *(Case Western Reserve University Archives photo)*

A bustling Public Square is packed with streetcars, automobiles, and pedestrians making their way through the city on a fall afternoon in 1932. The trolley in the foreground allowed people to walk between the front and rear cars. This scene shows streetcars on two of the loops running clockwise. *(Cleveland Press photo, Jim Toman Collection)*

In early 1931 the new store for the Higbee Company is nearing completion. The store would open to the public in September. *(Cleveland* Press *photo, Jim Toman Collection)*

The company had originally been called Hower and Higbee and was located on Superior Avenue just west of Public Square. In 1902 Edward Higbee shortened the name to the Higbee Company and eight years later, due to the need for more space, moved the store's headquarters to a much larger building at Euclid Avenue and East 13th Street. Because the business continued to prosper, then president Asa Shiverick committed the department store to the Tower group and to Public Square. Newspaper accounts at the time said that the company's return to the Square helped to "attract the eyes of the whole world to the Square."

In committing $10 million to build the new store, the largest retail facility constructed in the country in 20 years, the company hoped to provide a luxurious shopping experience for the general public in an intimate and comfortable atmosphere that resembled a private club. When the 13-story emporium opened its doors at 9:00 a.m. on its first day, visitors were treated to an interior replete with beveled glass, leather-appointed lounges, rich wood paneling, and modern lighting. All day long, throngs passed through the doors to explore the new store and its $5 million worth of merchandise. By the end of the day 359,079 people, nearly 40% of the city's population, had poured into the department store. Contemporary commentators marveled at the vastness of the Higbee store and saw its opening as one of the key events in Cleveland merchandising history.

Not only was the Higbee Company's grand opening at Public Square significant in drawing area residents to the town's center, but the building completed the architectural development of the southwest quadrant of the Square. When officials dedicated the Tower Group a year earlier, a gaping hole in the ground just east of the Terminal Tower had still existed. Higbee's exterior design and materials blended well with those of the other buildings in the complex, and the Higbee Company building served to balance the Terminal Tower with the Hotel Cleveland. As part of the "city within a city," the store added a feeling of permanence to the city's hub and attracted people to the center of Cleveland.

Not to be outdone by its downtown neighbor, officials of the May Company had also developed plans for expanding and refurbishing its flagship store. In its quest to remain Ohio's largest department store, the company added two stories to its Public Square building. The new floors would allow the executive offices and the inventory area to be relocated to the new seventh and eighth levels, freeing up space below for more retail displays. The new floors added 200,000 square feet of space, giving the structure a total of one million square feet of retail space. Work on the two-story addition began in February 1931. Graham, Anderson, Probst and White served as the architects, adding another chapter to their architectural legacy on Public Square.

The improvements in the store included ventilating equipment, escalators, restrooms, new lighting, and a general interior redecoration. On the outside, new display windows and a marquee stretching across the entire front of the store marked the updated May Company facility. The classic clock and parapet, which had been removed from the sixth story to make way for the addition, was repositioned atop the new eighth floor.

(The May Company actually had two clocks atop its downtown store. The second one was on its Ontario Street building. Due to structural problems, that clock had to be removed on April 30, 1948. While it lost that clock, Public Square gained another one on December 28, 1947, when the owners of the Williamson Building installed a stylized version above its main entranceway on Euclid Avenue at the East Roadway.)

When the new bronze-molded doors to the building swung open

To keep pace with its downtown rivals, and in particular Higbee's, May's added two floors to its downtown store in 1931. In front of the building a company bus drops off shoppers from the May's parking garage on Lakeside Avenue. *(Cleveland Press Collection of the Cleveland State University Libraries)*

on November 9, 1931, a large crowd was waiting. Most of the people, of course, had come by trolley, but May Company officials, aware of the growing popularity of the automobile, also operated a parking garage on Lakeside Avenue and Ontario Street and provided a free bus ride between the garage and the store.

The May Company developed its relationship with its customers in many different ways. One of them evolved into a longtime Cleveland tradition. When the financial constraints of the Great Depression in 1929 prevented the city from being able to install its Christmas tree in Public Square, a local nursery stepped in to fill the gap. Then in 1932 and 1933, the furrier I. J. Fox provided the holiday greenery. But beginning in 1934, the May Company took charge of the holiday decoration, and continued to provide the downtown tree until wartime austerity temporarily halted the tradition.

Yuletide arches decorate the northeast quadrant during the holiday season in 1927. In the background is the Ulmer Building (later to be named 33 Public Square). *(Cleveland Picture Collection of Cleveland Public Library)*

For much of the 20th century Clevelanders have been drawn to Public Square during the holiday season, not just to shop, but to take in the Christmas lights there. In this 1930s scene, a tree dominates the northeast quadrant. *(Cleveland* Press *Collection of the Cleveland State University Libraries)*

Another holiday custom on the Square was born in this era as well. The annual Christmas parade and tree lighting became an integral part of Clevelanders' seasonal celebrations. In 1934, for instance, about 50,000 people watched a night time parade which was sponsored by the *Cleveland Press.* The festivities featured the lighting of the tree, a tradition that has lasted to this day. In 1935 the parade was moved to daylight hours, and a crowd, estimated at 150,000, congregated along Euclid Avenue and on Public Square—especially around the Soldiers' and Sailors' Monument on the southeast quadrant. Beginning at East 21st Street, the parade wound its way to the eastern part of the Square. When Santa Claus's sleigh reached the Square, the lights on the huge Christmas tree in the northeast corner were turned on.

Civic planners and other area residents also used the city's "front lawn" for numerous other festivities and events during this period, too. Especially significant were the many war-related gatherings on the Square. During the fighting of World War II, many gathered at the northwest quadrant of the Square to dedicate the Cleveland War Service Center. An estimated 25,000 people came to hear speeches about the gravity of the country's fight against the Axis powers. According to *Plain Dealer* accounts, the War Service Center was also dedicated as a place to remind area residents to buy war bonds and stamps to "wipe the gloating smiles off the faces of the Japanese." Workers who constructed the unimposing structure painted it white, according to Mayor Frank Lausche, to indicate the purity of the American effort against aggression. Beside the structure a "Flame of Patriotism" was lighted as a reminder to passers by that the nation was at conflict. It remained lighted until the end of the war.

Public Square held other patriotic displays as well. In 1942, the Cleveland Chamber of Commerce installed on the southwest quadrant a Court of Flags of the United Nations. They were positioned along the diagonal walkway leading away from the entrance to the Union Terminal. The 28 steel poles and the national flags which flew from them were another patriotic sign of the city's solidarity with the nation's war effort.

Only two months after the War Service Center's dedication, another symbolic moment in Cleveland history took place on the town green. On October 7, 1942, Cleveland Electric Illuminating Company donated to Cuyahoga County's War Scrap Metal Pile the electric machine patented by Charles F. Brush that had first provided the city light in 1893. Called the Brush Dynamo, the 1,200-pound museum piece had been

Patriotic symbols graced the Square during the Second World War. On the southwest quadrant a "Court of Flags" from the allied nations flank the Moses Cleaveland statue. *(Cleveland* Press *Collection of the Cleveland State University Libraries)*

The temporary War Service Center, which occupied space on the northwest quadrant during World War II, served as the focal point for the local patriotic effort. It was dismantled soon after the conflict ended. *(Cleveland* Press *Collection of the Cleveland State University Libraries)*

on exhibit at the C.E.I. Avon plant. It was more than just another contribution to the area's home war efforts. The dynamo had provided the Forest City with its first electric light almost 50 years before. Its donation was intended to encourage area residents to give up their own surplus metals to the drive. C.E.I offered the electric machine on the first day of a two-week drive, during which organizers hoped to raise 50 million pounds of scrap metal. Soon, other donations followed: a family sword from the Civil War, iron beds of sons who were serving in the war, an Austrian rifle, and some refrigerators.

When the Nazis surrendered in May 1945, the War Production Board lifted the restrictions that had been imposed upon city lighting. Bulbs in downtown marquees, building displays, and outdoor advertising once again lit up Cleveland. V-E celebrations, however, were restrained, as the Pacific war continued. Spirits changed dramatically on August 15, 1945, when word came that the Japanese had surrendered. People reacted with great emotion, many in tears as they listened to the Square's loudspeaker deliver the great news outside the War Service Center. That evening, confetti and paper streamers swirled about the buildings on Public Square and along Euclid Avenue, and people took their convertibles from storage and circled again and again around the city green.

Shortly following the impromptu celebration, Clevelanders on September 11 again convened downtown for the city's official V-J parade, which drew about 300,000 jubilant onlookers to the Public Square area. The victory parade started at St. Clair Avenue and East 6th Street, headed west to Ontario Street, south through the Square, east on Euclid Avenue to East 18th Street and eventually back to the reviewing stand in front of the Public Library on Superior Avenue. Members of the V-J Day Committee of the Joint Veterans Commission of Cuyahoga County aimed to make it "the greatest parade Cleveland ever has had," and those who went to

The War Service Center on the northwest quadrant was the focal point of many patriotic events during the Second World War. The Tom L. Johnson monument stands in the middle of "the nation's finest." (Cleveland Press *Collection of the Cleveland State University Libraries*)

the early evening parade were likely not disappointed. The weather cooperated, and the celebration was truly joyous.

Eight months later, one of the heroes of the American war effort was greeted to a civic celebration of mammoth proportions. An estimated 500,000 Clevelanders welcomed General Dwight D. Eisenhower to the area on April 12, 1946. After stopping at Lakewood High School, the general, riding in an open car, was greeted at Public Square by swarms of people and a hail of ticker tape. Postwar patriotism continued into May, as the 1946 Memorial Day celebration held in the Court of Flags drew 25,000 for the ceremony honoring those Clevelanders who had lost their lives in the war.

Aside from the many war-related gatherings that graced the convergence of Ontario Street and Superior Avenue, the city's hub during this period witnessed other significant moments as well. One example occurred in April 1939, when for a night Cleveland's downtown area resembled conditions of an air raid when the lights dimmed. Instead of people dashing for cover, however, they stood patiently awaiting the hoisting of a replica of Brush's first arc lamp. Organizers attached the lamp to the flagpole on the southwest quadrant. The 135th Field Artillery cannon then shot a thundering volley, and a moment later, a feeble light flickered above the Square.

Presidential visits to the city were always attended by significant amounts of civic hoopla, and Public Square usually played a role in their events. On October 2, 1930, President Herbert Hoover visited the city. His entourage traveled down Euclid Avenue to Public Square and from there to Public Auditorium where he spoke to an assembled crowd about his hopes for better economic times. His successor in office, Franklin Delano Roosevelt, also visited the city. In August 1936 he also traveled down Euclid Avenue and through Public Square on his way to visit the city's Great Lakes Exposition on the lakefront. Both visits saw thousands of onlookers gathered in the Square to catch a glimpse of the national leaders.

Historic occasions also were typically celebrated on the city green. However, the city's sesquicentennial ceremonies in 1946 were largely centered on the Mall. One part, though, on July 21, included a two-mile long parade with 50 floats which began in Public Square and then continued out Euclid Avenue to East Boulevard. Tens of thousands gathered in the Square and downtown for the event.

Sporting events have also provided moments which beckoned people to the town green. In the late 1930s, for example, fans gathered on the northwest quadrant to listen to baseball results of Indians' games via loudspeakers on the Cleveland Electric Illuminating

In an era before large-screen video monitors and cable channels, Cleveland baseball fans could catch the latest developments of an Indians' game by listening to the loudspeaker affixed on the Cleveland Electric Illuminating (C.E.I.) Building. This photo dates from 1938. *(Cleveland* Press *Collection of the Cleveland State University Libraries)*

Building. One particular event in 1938 was designed to publicize the Terminal Tower. Attempting to break the world record for an altitude baseball catch, some members of the Cleveland Indians on August 20 were the center of attention for 10,000 who gathered around the southwest quadrant of the Square. Stationed 708 feet above Public Square, Tribe third baseman Ken Keltner, launched the baseballs. Third-string catcher Hank Helf made the first catch. On Keltner's sixth throw, Frankie Pytlak, another catcher, cleanly snared the ball. It was estimated that the balls were falling 138 miles per hour. With their catches, both surpassed the old record for the feat, which had been set in 1908 by Gabby Street, who caught a baseball dropped from the top of the 555-foot Washington Monument.

In October 1948 city leaders chose Public Square as the site for an even more joyful celebration to honor the World Series champion Cleveland Indians. On October 12 the team's train from Boston arrived around 8:30 a.m. at the Union Terminal, at which point the players were escorted to 20 open cars waiting on Public Square. A crowd, variously estimated at between 200,000 and 500,000 area residents, heartily cheered the likes of Lou Boudreau, Larry Doby, Gene Bearden, Ken Keltner, and Bill Veeck during a parade that began in front of the Terminal Tower and proceeded five slow miles along Euclid Avenue to University Circle. The people lining the avenue so crowded the cavalcade that the busy street turned into a one-lane roadway.

The triumphant 1948 Cleveland Indians make their way from the Terminal Tower down Euclid Avenue amid a throng of cheering fans. A car carrying two key elements of that World Series-clinching squad, Lou Boudreau (on the left) and owner Bill Veeck (right) enjoy the festivities. *(Cleveland Press Collection of the Cleveland State University Libraries)*

Public Square has not only been a place for celebration, however. It served as the setting for numerous protests and the site of much debate, too. Throughout the 1930s local Communists and Communist sympathizers used Public Square's rostrum to deliver their message and in particular to commemorate Workers' Day every May 1. One meeting of Communists in 1930, for instance, was charged by police on horseback until the group dispersed. A few hundred demonstrators, most of whom were unemployed, had convened to march in support of a petition for relief from the Community Fund. After three hours of speeches near the statue of Tom L. Johnson on the southwest quadrant, a speaker mounted the rostrum nearby, and pointing to the American flag waving in the breeze atop the Federal Building, shouted, "down with this flag and up with this one." At that moment he raised a red flag, and police charged the group, forcing it to disband. Nobody was hurt in the exchange between police and protestors. Police sometimes had their own sense of just how far the quadrant's free speech tradition could go. City leaders were also apprehensive at the May Day parades the political left sponsored, and they often mobilized the police department to be on guard for disturbances. Throughout the economically troubled decade, radical orators near the Johnson statue spoke almost daily about the values of socialism and communism.

An orator on the northwest quadrant's free speech rostrum (just to the right of the light post) addresses a winter crowd during the Depression. The rostrum was installed in 1916 to honor the liberal ideals of Cleveland Mayor Tom L. Johnson, but its popularity grew as the times became progressively more troubled. *(Bruce Young Collection)*

The Depression era on Public Square was ripe with many gatherings of people eager for economic change. These rallies were often sponsored by local Socialist or Communist parties and drew thousands of Clevelanders to the Square. *(Cleveland Picture Collection of Cleveland Public Library)*

The period between 1920-1950 was a boon for the city in many ways. During this time, Cleveland's population grew to an all-time high of 914,808, and it reached its largest physical size (the last annexation of unincorporated land took place in 1932). Despite the Depression, area voters approved public projects like Municipal Stadium that significantly enriched their civic lives. It rose on the lakefront during a time of economic woe. Baseball's Indians captured a world championship, and a young professional team, the Browns, captured the hearts of Clevelanders with consecutive AAFC titles. Cleveland had earned nationwide respect for its continuing successes in urban planning. Most importantly, though, the Union Station complex, which had taken over a decade to complete and which was Cleveland's largest urban construction program to date, had significantly altered both the layout and skyline of downtown. It would leave a legacy rich in many ways: transportation center, retail hub, architectural landmark, and popular attraction.

The vitality of that legacy would be tested in the years ahead.

In Cleveland, "all paths lead to the Square." Though Euclid and Superior avenues are well lighted, Public Square and the streets are mostly empty on this fall evening in the 1940s. *(Blaine Hays Collection)*

The Doldrums
1950 - 1979

At mid-century the City of Cleveland achieved its all-time greatest population, 914,808.

The increase over 1940, however, was modest: a mere 4% growth. Considering the fact that the war years had seen significant relocation of workers to the nation's industrialized urban areas, it was clear that the boom years for the Cleveland were past. In fact, the population in 1950 was only 1.5% greater than it had been in 1930. As a result, Cleveland's rank slipped a notch, to seventh place on the list of the nation's largest cities. Stagnation had replaced growth.

In many ways Public Square reflected the demographic picture. Little had changed since 1930, the only major structural difference being the loss of the old court house. The collapse of the Van Sweringen empire and of the banks which had fallen with it had recast the investment spirit of the city from an enthusiastic progressivism to a risk-avoiding conservatism.

While these signs were not promising, in 1950 the sights and sounds of downtown seemed much as they had been. Downtown was still the region's shopping center, and it still boasted six department stores: Higbee's, Bailey's, and May's at the Square; and Taylor's, Halle's, and Sterling's up the avenue. Downtown had even added a few retail stores during the early post-war period. A modern Bond's clothing store went up at Euclid and East Ninth in 1947, and in 1948 a new Woolworth's store replaced the former headquarters building of Central National Bank on lower Euclid Avenue, west of East Fourth Street. People also still came downtown for the movies. Along Euclid Avenue, the Mall, Embassy, Hippodrome, Stillman, Allen, Ohio, State, and Palace theaters were still doing good business. And people still came downtown by streetcar, although by 1950 the steel-wheeled vehicles were rapidly becoming extinct.

Social rituals remained much as they had been. Often friends, planning a day of shopping or a night at the movies, would meet on Public Square, or in less clement weather, in one of the concourses of Cleveland Union Terminal, which as a train station never closed its doors. The outing might with start off with a visit to Harvey's on the Union Terminal concourse for a cherry coke or a lemon phosphate. Or it might include a break in Higbee's or May's basement stores for a thick frosted malted. If a full day's outing was the plan, it might include lunch at Higbee's Silver Grill or May's Mayfair Room, or Halle's Geranium Room, or perhaps a quick bite at the popular Clark's, Mill's, or Mayflower restaurants on lower Euclid Avenue, or at the Forum on East Ninth Street. If the occasion was a night out at the movies, it might be capped with an imaginative ice cream concoction at Boukair's or with a cocktail at the Alpine Village in Playhouse Square. Things downtown indeed seemed much the same for the second generation coming of age after the Terminal Tower had first punctuated the downtown skyline.

But while on the surface all seemed much as it had been, and while the habits and customs of the community had not yet greatly altered, the perception of constancy was more illusion than reality. Change is inevitable, and though it may have been less dramatic during the 1950s than it had been in the exciting 1920s, and though its manifestations may have been less immediately felt, it was nonetheless underway. Subtly but surely the fortunes and the face of Cleveland's center were about to experience

A packed Public Square bustles with streetcars, buses, automobiles, and pedestrians. It is 1950, and streetcars had only four more years before they would give way entirely to rubber-tired vehicles. *(Cleveland* Press *Collection of the Cleveland State University Libraries)*

profound changes.

Perhaps one reason that the changes getting underway in the 1950s seemed less dramatic than in the past was that they were being framed more by subtraction than by addition. A prime example of this trend came in 1953 when the first real change in the wall of familiar buildings enfolding Public Square took place--the result of demolition.

In 1929, after the Cleveland Chamber of Commerce had relocated from its 1897 vintage headquarters on the northeast quadrant of the Square to new offices in the Terminal Tower, Western Reserve University purchased the Chamber's old home to be the downtown campus for its Cleveland College division. At first, Cleveland College thrived at its Public Square location. In fact, in 1947 the university even commissioned plans for constructing an annex behind the Public Square facility. Enrollment was surging, largely occasioned by World War II veterans taking advantage of the educational opportunities provided by the G.I. Bill. By 1950, however, enrollment pressures slowed, and the university found that not only did it not need new space downtown, but that it also was facing a surplus of classroom seats at its University Circle campus. Economics clearly dictated that operations be consolidated on the main campus, which meant that the university would no longer need the old Chamber of Commerce building.

The university did not have to look far for a buyer. The building's next door neighbor, the Society for Savings, wanted the property--but not the building. In a time when automobile sales were skyrocketing and when suburban facilities were being built with large parking lots, downtown businesses were increasingly recognizing the importance of providing parking options for their patrons. The Chamber site seemed ideal for a parking lot to accommodate bank customers, so in September 1953 the Society for Savings purchased the property, and two months later demolition got underway. The Society lot became Public Square's second surface parking area, balancing the one on the other edge of the Square's northern boundary, where the old court house had once stood. At least the Society for Savings had the good grace to hide its lot by enclosing it with a high brick wall.

Small changes were also happening on the Square, again by subtraction. Two of the Square's military memorials disappeared. The carriage bearing the Civil War cannon had deteriorated to such an extent that the cannon could easily have toppled onto an unsuspecting passer-by. It was removed in 1949. Then in 1951, the city decided to relocate the cannon from the War of 1812 to Gordon Park where it could be displayed alongside the statue of Commodore Perry.

The use of valuable Public Square area property for parking purposes illustrated just how important the automobile had become in the post-war period. In 1946, Cleveland Transit System's (CTS) streetcars and buses had carried their all-time high ridership, 493 million. By 1953 the public transit agency had lost 146 million of those passengers, a loss of nearly 30%. Those riders had become drivers.

In 1953 Public Square experienced its first major change in over 20 years. The old Chamber of Commerce Building (right) was demolished to make way for a surface parking lot just off the northeast quadrant. *(Cleveland* Press *Collection of the Cleveland State University Libraries)*

The changing patterns of public travel preferences were, of course, being addressed by the Cleveland Transit System (CTS), the public agency which in 1942 had taken over control of the city's public transit operations from the Cleveland Railway Company. In 1946 the agency had decided to abandon its extensive surface streetcar system whose operating efficiency was being severely compromised by the increase in automobile traffic. Chicago consultant Charles E. DeLeuw had recommended that streetcars be replaced by rubber-tire vehicles on the surface and by a single crosstown rail rapid transit line which would include a downtown subway. All along the rapid transit line, a network of feeder bus routes would funnel riders to the rapid for a fast trip downtown. CTS and Cleveland City Council approved the plan, and beginning in 1946, just as rapidly as it could secure replacement vehicles, CTS began to convert its streetcar lines to rubber-tire operation. Cleveland's last streetcar line, running from Public Square via Madison Avenue to Rocky River Drive in Lakewood ended revenue service on January 23, 1954.

A huge crowd turned out for the last streetcar ride in Cleveland history on January 24, 1954. Here, people wait to board the Madison Avenue line that day in front of the Terminal Tower. *(Cleveland Transit System photo, Blaine Hays Collection)*

Community leaders decided that after 95 years of faithful service to the community, streetcars deserved a proper sendoff, and so Sunday, January 24, 1954, was designated as a "Farewell to Streetcars" day. Sponsored by the Cleveland *Press*, the event offered interested Greater Clevelanders a free final streetcar ride from Public Square through the Detroit-Superior Bridge subway to West 65th Street and back. CTS officials, however, had underestimated the response this nostalgic event generated, and they had to scurry to add more streetcars to serve the throng of more than 10,000 hardy souls who braved bitterly cold weather for this final chapter in Cleveland's (and Ohio's) streetcar history. The line of waiting passengers snaked all around the Square's southwest quadrant, many in the crowd queuing patiently for hours before they finally had their chance to board. Finally, at 3:52 p.m., Cleveland's last streetcar squealed its way out of the Square onto West Superior Avenue, and then disappeared into the gloom of the Detroit Superior Subway. An era had come to an end.

The end of streetcar operations made possible several changes to Public Square. Increasing automobile traffic had made the four-lane stretch of Ontario Street through Public Square into a bottleneck. With the streetcar tracks no longer an obstacle, and by trimming back the sidewalks on both sides of the street, engineers were able to widen Ontario by 17 feet and add two more traffic lanes. By September 1954 Ontario's widening had been completed and the streetcars' shiny steel rails covered over by asphalt.

The overhead wire network, however, remained in place. That was because the Cleveland Transit System had replaced several of the streetcar lines with trackless trolleys. These hybrid vehicles looked like buses, but though rubber tired, they were electrically powered, with two roof-mounted trolley poles drawing and returning current via a two-wire overhead system. Non-polluting and quiet, trackless trolleys were popular with transit operators at the time. Altogether eight trackless trolley lines looped downtown around three of the Square's quadrant (no lines used the southeast quadrant). So while the streetcars' tracks were buried, the overhead wire network was in fact nearly doubled.

A third change came in response to a request by Cleveland Mayor Anthony J. Celebrezze. He felt that the 53-year-old pagoda waiting stations were out of keeping with the modern image the city wished to cultivate, so he prevailed upon CTS to install new shelters of more contemporary design. CTS complied, and 1955 saw the installation of four aluminum and plate glass waiting rooms on the Square. While the replacement shelters were certainly of modern functional design, they did little to enhance the architectural character of the Square.

Also added that year was an information kiosk jointly operated by the transit system and the Cleveland Convention and Visitors Bureau. The small brick and glass structure was located in the southwest quadrant near the intersection of Ontario Street and the South Roadway. When the structure opened in January 1955, the City would not grant permission for it to carry any signage, since that was considered inappropriate for the Square. As the Convention Bureau rightly argued, however, it seemed unlikely that many visitors would make their way to the kiosk for city information if they could not determine the purpose of the building. Eventually the City relented, and in July 1955 the kiosk had a "Welcome to Cleveland" sign attached to it roof.

The modern shelters and the kiosk were joined in 1957 by a modern-looking but rather inconsequential band shell in the southwest quadrant of the Square. The translucent fiberglass structure became the venue for periodic band and choral offerings, particularly

In 1957 a plexiglass bandshell was installed on the southwest quadrant of Public Square. Perhaps these modest beginnings lay the groundwork for the very popular Cleveland Orchestra performances of the 1990s. *(Cleveland* Press *Collection of the Cleveland State University Libraries)*

during the Christmas shopping season. The shell was dedicated to the memory of William Ganson Rose, civic leader and foremost chronicler of the city's history, who had died that year. (The band shell was removed in 1974.)

In 1955 CTS's new rapid transit line began operations. Cleveland Union Terminal (CUT) served as the central station on the line, which ran 13.1 miles from Windermere in the east to West 117th Street in the west. To accommodate the expected surge of passengers for the new line, CTS had built two station areas in the Terminal, one in the central concourse and one in the western traction concourse. Despite high hopes for the rapid transit line, however, its projected ridership failed to materialize. In 1956, the first full year of rapid operation, a total of 14.7 million rides were counted, only about 36% of what transit consultants had projected. CTS officials, however, were not unduly worried. They anticipated that the projected numbers would be achieved only when the rapid transit line was connected into the downtown distributor subway. The subway would make taking the rapid more attractive for those who were working in the stores and offices located away from Public Square. They would not have to transfer to get to their destinations.

Plans for the subway were well underway. The Cuyahoga County commissioners had placed a $35 million subway bond issue on the November 1953 ballot, and voters had overwhelmingly supported the issue. The planned subway was to form a loop, from Cleveland Union Terminal to West Sixth Street, then east beneath Superior Avenue to East 13th Street, south to Huron Road, and then back to the Terminal. Besides the CUT station and three other downtown intersections, there would have been a subway station beneath Public Square, at Superior Avenue and the East Roadway.

This aerial view of Public Square at mid-century shows the downtown green still dressed in her 1930s garb. The only change is the loss of the old Cuyahoga County Court House on the site of the parking lot (bottom right). *(Cleveland Press Collection of the Cleveland State University Libraries)*

Just how successful the subway might have been in attracting new transit riders, how its construction might have affected the Public Square, or whether it would have injected a new vitality into a declining downtown will never be known. In November 1959, the Board of County Commissioners, at the urging of County Engineer Albert Porter, decided not to issue the subway bonds. Porter had successfully argued that public transportation should no longer be the priority in county spending, that the increase in automobile ownership and use demanded that county resources be allocated to improving the area's roads and bridges. The commissioners' decision unfortunately failed to take into consideration the potential of the subway for spurring downtown development. Thus an opportunity to give downtown a boost was lost. This was the second major subway plan to be stymied.

While the subway was lost, some other building plans did materialize. In July 1955 the Cleveland Electric Illuminating Company announced plans for a new Public Square headquarters building, immediately west of its existing offices at 75 Public Square. The site had been a surface parking lot ever since 1935 when the old Cuyahoga County Court House, which had previously occupied the property, was razed. The Illuminating Building was to be Public Square's first new structure since the opening of the Higbee Company store in 1931. It was also to be the city's first example of the glass-curtain-walled modernist skyscraper, a style which had its American debut in 1952 with New York City's Lever House.

Groundbreaking for the 22-story Illuminating Building at 55 Public Square took place on February 1, 1956. The building rose 300 feet, and its glass-paneled walls and white marble vertical trim served to both reflect and shed light onto the northwest quadrant below. The architects, Carson and Lundin of New York City, were mindful of the need to provide the new building with adequate parking, and they thoughtfully situated an attached seven-story garage to the rear of the building, invisible from Public Square. By setting the tower itself back from the roadway, the planners were also able to create a

The first major architectural change in the Public Square neighborhood since the opening of the Cleveland Union Terminal was the Illuminating Building (left), dedicated in 1958. Known today as 55 Public Square, it was Cleveland's first building in the modernist style. *(Perry Cragg photo, Jim Toman Collection)*

small plaza at the Public Square side of the building, in a way extending the public space provided by the Square itself. The first floor of the building contained a electric appliance consumer center and a restaurant. The tower greeted its first tenant (Kaiser Aluminum) in November 1957. The Illuminating Company did not move into its new headquarters until January 1958. Formal dedication of the skyscraper followed, on February 18, 1958.

Public Square gained twice from the new building. It not only provided the Square with a bright example of contemporary architecture, it also filled in a structural gap in the perimeter of the Square, and in doing so effaced an ugly surface parking lot. Many Clevelanders hoped that the new building, the first major addition to the downtown skyline since the Terminal Tower opened almost 30 years before, heralded a return to the development dynamism of the first third of the century. Those hopes were premature.

When the U.S. Department of Commerce announced its census figures for 1960, the city of Cleveland proper had registered a drop in numbers. Its population had declined to 876,050. At the same time, the population of Cuyahoga County had registered a 19% increase. For the first time, the population in the county's suburban communities exceeded that of the central city. Commercial interests had been quick to respond to the suburban growth. During the 1950s five large suburban shopping centers had opened: Eastgate, Westgate, Southgate, Parmatown, and Golden Gate. Conveniently located and surrounded by ample parking lots, these developments were not long in impacting on the fortunes of downtown Cleveland.

One of the first blows that the suburban developments delivered to downtown's retail preeminence came on December 16, 1961. That was the day that the William Taylor and Sons department store on Euclid Avenue at East Sixth Street closed its doors. Taylor's had actually become part of the May Company back in 1939, but it had continued to operate under its original name. Declining sales made two May Company outlets downtown untenable, and so after 91 years of retail operations, the Taylor name faded into history.

Just four months later, the Bailey Company store on Ontario and Prospect followed suit. In 1958, when new owners had taken over the Bailey Company, they were not without concern about the future of downtown retailing. Putting their worries aside, however, the new owners decided to commit $1 million to storewide renovation. The store's interior was brightened, and the aging exterior was sheathed with blue-tinted steel panels, giving the building a modern, if somewhat garish, appearance. Despite the makeover, sales continued to slip, and the owners decided to throw in the towel. On March 22, 1962, after 81 years of downtown merchandising, Bailey's joined Taylor's on memory row.

Bailey's was the second downtown department store to close. It failed despite the considerable investment that its owners made in modernizing both the interior and the exterior of the store. *(Cleveland Press Collection of the Cleveland State University Libraries)*

With Bailey's closing, Public Square's department store cluster was reduced to just May's and Higbee's. May Company officials were quick to react to the closing of Bailey's. May's officers realized that in an automobile-oriented age, their downtown store had to offer the convenience of parking to its patrons, or its future would be bleak. With that objective in mind, May's bought the Bailey property as the site for a new parking garage. In April 1963 demolition on the Bailey store got underway. Three months later construction began on May's Parkade, an 11-story parking facility for 720 cars. The facility was finished in time for the Christmas 1964 shopping season. The Parkade made parking for May's shoppers very convenient. Various levels of the garage provided direct access to the department store's shopping floors. While the new garage provided convenience, however, its sharply spiraling exit ramps proved harrowing for timid drivers. Many younger motorists, though, seemed to enjoy the challenge posed by the tight turning radius.

Even before the city had lost the two department stores, Cleveland city officials had become cognizant that the downtown sector was in need of redevelopment and reinvestment. The chosen vehicle of the time was to target a specific area of the city as a renewal zone, and then using the power of eminent domain, to clear away existing buildings and offer the prepared sites to developers at attractive prices. Generously supported by federal dollars, urban renewal, as the concept was then known, offered older cash-strapped cities the opportunity to challenge the tides of urban decay.

In 1960 City of Cleveland officials, spurred on by the editorial voice of the Cleveland *Press,* committed itself to its first downtown urban renewal project, Erieview. The selected zone originally was to encompass 125 acres of downtown Cleveland, stretching roughly from Lakeside Avenue south to Chester Avenue and from East Sixth Street west to East 17th Street. East Ninth Street would be the central corridor for the renewal district. At the time, East Ninth Street, north of Chester Avenue, was lined by a shabby collection of worn out buildings with the exception of the St. John the Evangelist Cathedral and the East Ohio Building (1958) at Superior Avenue and the sparkling new home of the *Press* at Lakeside Avenue. Some critics of the plan felt that the *Press's* enthusiastic support for it may have been more than a little self serving.

This aerial view shows the Park Center (now Reserve Square) apartments under construction. Creating a downtown residential zone was one of the goals of the Erieview plan, an aim which was only partially achieved. *(Cleveland* Press *Collection of the Cleveland State University Libraries)*

The outline of the Erieview plan was the product of the renowned architectural and urban planning firm of I. M. Pei and Associates of New York City. Its details were unveiled to the public in November 1960. In that same month Cleveland voters approved bond issues to provide seed money for the Erieview project, as well as for renovating and expanding the city's cramped convention facilities located in Public Auditorium and its underground annex.

As a result of these commitments, hundreds of millions of dollars in both public and private funding were ultimately directed towards redeveloping the Erieview sector. The original centerpiece of the Erieview project, the Erieview Tower, a 524-foot, 40-story skyscraper designed by Harrison and Abramovitz of New York City, rose near East 12th Street. Its frontage facing East Ninth Street was laid out as a plaza with fountains and a reflecting pool. The tower (now called the Tower at Erieview) opened in 1964. (The plaza was replaced by the Galleria shopping mall in 1987).

The eventual Erieview configuration, however, only slightly resembled the original Pei design. The size of the project was also cut back. The time line for the Erieview development ultimately extended over almost 30 years, and its individual components were designed to reflect changing times and interests.

The Erieview plan rebuilt the East Ninth Street corridor. To the left is the Erieview Tower, completed in 1964. To the west of East Ninth Street two other buildings are under construction. In the foreground is the new federal office building, and one block south is the new Cuyahoga Savings Building. *(Cleveland* Press *Collection of the Cleveland State University Libraries)*

While Erieview can certainly be credited with injecting new life into the East Ninth Street district and into the creation of what became Cleveland's financial sector, the new buildings there were strictly utilitarian. Most of them lacked even basic people-oriented spaces, such as dining areas or shops. As a result Erieview did little to attract people to the city's core, nor did it do anything to focus redevelopment interest in the Public Square neighborhood. It would be more than 20 years from the time that the Erieview plan was announced before the heart of the city would again recapture its earlier pre-eminence as the center of downtown redevelopment.

While the Erieview project brought no changes to Public Square, it did contribute to the modernization of the city's other downtown green. While Public Square remained in its dowdy 1930s dress, the Mall took on a fresh new look. Mall B, the section between St. Clair and Lakeside avenues, was excavated for the underground expansion of the convention center. Following construction, the roof of the new exhibit space became the new Mall B. It was completely replanted, and its center was graced by a reflecting pool and fountains, a gift of the Leonard C. Hanna Fund. At the same time Mall A, the southernmost portion of the green, between St. Clair and Rockwell avenues and diagonally across from the northeastern quadrant of the Square, also received a makeover. There the City installed a memorial fountain and sculpture, *Peace Rising from the Flames of War* by sculptor Marshall Fredericks. Largely paid for by modest individual contributions and a collection taken up among the school children of the city, the memorial honored those Greater Clevelanders who had lost their lives in World War II and in the Korean conflict. The redesign of the two Mall spaces was completed in 1964.

A few changes did take place around the central green during the 1960s. While not directly on the Square, new construction was undertaken by Public Square's most venerable occupant in 1961. That year Old Stone Church began construction on a new parish house. Wedged between the church and the Standard Building, its main entrance was on Ontario Street. The new facility gave the church a modern and enlarged community center. The parish house was completed and ready for the congregation's use in 1964.

A more noticeable change occurred in 1962 when the Sheraton Cleveland Hotel (Hotel Cleveland had been purchased by the Sheraton chain in 1958) was renovated and expanded with a new ballroom/banquet facility and parking garage. The hotel's original 1000 rooms became 758. While reduced in number, the rooms were increased in size. The ballroom and garage were built on the western side of the hotel, away from Public Square, facing Superior Avenue. The hotel operator proudly proclaimed that the ballroom/banquet facility was the largest between New York City and Chicago.

In 1963 the short chapter of the trackless trolley in Cleveland came to an end. The last lines to use Public Square for their downtown turning loop were the Hough, Superior, and Wade Park routes. They ran for the last time on April 12 (the final three trackless trolley lines, which did not use the Square for a turning loop, quit on June 14). With the end of trackless trolley service, crews were able to free Public Square from a plethora of overhead power lines and support cables.

Across Superior Avenue from the Sheraton Cleveland Hotel another set of changes was getting underway. In 1965 the buildings facing the northwest quadrant of Public Square were given a facelift. Between the Marshall Building and the Public Square Building stood Public Square's shortest structure, a dilapidated three-story vestige from the 1880s. Over the years the small building had housed a variety of tenants, and for many years it had served as the ticket office for the old Lake Shore Electric interurban trolley line (it ceased operations in 1938). But more noticeably, the roof of the three-story building served as the base of a ten-story billboard, touting the taste of various bottom-shelf whiskeys.

The brief existence of the trackless trolley in Cleveland lasted from 1936-1963.
The two pictured here are on the overhead that served the St. Clair line. Old Stone
Church and the Society for Savings Building form the backdrop. *(Robert Runyon
photo, Bruce Young Collection)*

The billboard may have disguised the diminutive stature of the old building, but its vulgar commercialism somehow seemed an affront to the dignity which the city's center green deserved. Most, therefore applauded the announcement that the building and its billboard would be torn down, and in its place would rise a 14-story addition to the Marshall Building. At the same time, both the Marshall and the Public Square buildings were given more contemporary facades. In addition to their new outer skins and windows, the buildings also received new names. The Marshall Building became the One Public Square Building, and its frequently renamed neighbor to the north was given yet another as the 33 Public Square Building.

The 1960s were a time when the value of architectural preservation was not yet popular, and so most people saw the buildings' fresh fronts as a positive contribution to the perimeter of the Square. And while some may have felt a tinge of regret that the familiar old faces of the Marshall and Mohawk buildings were hidden away, the demolition of the liquor billboard could only be construed as an improvement.

In 1966 the Cleveland Convention and Visitors Bureau proposed building a hospitality center in the middle of the northeast quadrant of the Square. The city's Fine Arts Advisory Committee raised immediate objections. Joseph McCullough, chairman of the committee, noted that "other cities are envious of our green spaces," in requesting that nothing be done in or to the Square without first conducting a complete study to determine its impact. While Cleveland clearly needed some spark, citizens were not willing for it to be struck in the Square. The Square may have become rundown, but it was still a special place to Clevelanders, and they were opposed to any loss of the public space that the Square offered.

This 1954 photo of Public Square shows the huge, multi-story billboard advertising alcohol between the Marshall and Public Square buildings off the northwest quadrant. To many, the huge sign and clock were an eyesore to the town green. *(Cleveland* Press *Collection of the Cleveland State University Libraries)*

The Marshall and Public Square buildings received a new facade in 1965. Gone was the old liquor sign, and the old building names as well. They emerged as the 1 and 33 Public Square buildings. *(Jim Toman photo)*

By 1970 the Square itself had stood largely unchanged for 40 years, since the last major makeover done in 1930 to coincide with the opening of the Cleveland Union Terminal complex. The Square had a tired look about it, mirroring the general lack of vibrancy that characterized downtown. For while Erieview added new office buildings and improved the city's skyline, the elements that were chiefly capable of drawing people to downtown--shopping and entertainment--were in dramatic decline.

As the 1960s came to an end, one after another of Cleveland's downtown movie houses along upper Euclid Avenue were shuttered. The Stillman Theater had been the first to close, in 1963. It was demolished to make way for a parking garage. A few years later the malaise spread to Playhouse Square itself as one theater marquee after another went dark. The Allen Theater closed in 1968, and the Ohio, State, and Palace theaters in 1969. Downtown also lost the third of its department stores. The Sterling-Lindner Company, one of the two Playhouse Square department stores, closed its doors on September 21, 1968. By the time the Christmas shopping season was winding down that year, the original Sterling and Welch portion of the consolidated store (it represented an amalgamation of the original Sterling and Welch Company with the W.B. Davis Company and the Lindner Company) had been reduced to rubble to make way for another parking lot. The demolition wrote "finis" to a long-standing Cleveland holiday tradition.

Ever since 1927 tens of thousands of Clevelanders had made visiting Sterling's a cheerful part of their holiday shopping plans to see the store's famous Christmas tree. The beautifully decorated Sterling's tree, located in the store's atrium, was billed as the nation's largest indoor Christmas tree.

Elsewhere downtown, signs were equally discouraging. The Pick Carter Hotel on Prospect Avenue at Huron Road, the Olmsted Hotel at Superior Avenue and East Ninth Street, and the Gaslight Inn (formerly the Allerton and then the Manger) all closed. All three were converted into subsidized apartment buildings. The loss of downtown hotel rooms was symptomatic of city without much to draw people to it.

Whether or not the subway might have prevented the decline in the fortunes of downtown, and particularly of Playhouse Square, cannot, of course, be known for certain. But had the subway been built as planned, the convenience of its Playhouse Square station might well have been a support for the theaters and stores located in the district.

In 1960 Sterling Lindner's famous annual Christmas tree stretches four stories high in the store's five-story atrium. The last of the popular holiday tradition was displayed in 1967. The store closed nine months later. *(Cleveland Press Collection of the Cleveland State University Libraries)*

The malaise that was affecting downtown was reflected in the city's 1970 census figures. Cleveland's population had dropped to 750,879, a 14.2% drop over the previous ten years. Cleveland had also slipped to tenth place among the nation's largest cities. The population's out-migration to suburbia had continued, and more suburban shopping malls with multi-screen movie theaters had been built. Downtown remained vigorous as an employment center, but its attractiveness for most other purposes had fallen precipitously. Bustling crowds of shoppers who had once crowded the downtown sidewalks throughout the day had largely become a lunch-time-only phenomenon.

Anyone walking through Cleveland Union Terminal could also see the signs of decline. As the celebrated Public Square facility reached its 40th birthday, its place as a railroad station was soon to fade into history. April 30, 1971, was the last day for Cleveland Union Terminal as an intercity passenger train station (as well as the last day for a while that the city would enjoy intercity passenger train service). When Amtrak, the nation's new intercity rail passenger operation restored service to the city October 31, 1975, its trains used a temporary station on the lakefront just west of East Ninth Street (the permanent Amtrak station on that site opened in 1977). After Amtrak's departure, the once bustling Cleveland Union Terminal had but one commuter train still using its track level. On January 14, 1977, the commuter service linking Cleveland and Youngstown made its final run, and the history of Cleveland Union Terminal as a railroad facility reached its final page (it still, however, served as the downtown rapid transit station). The historic significance of the Terminal Tower complex, however, was recognized in March 1976, when it joined other Public Square structures on the National Historic Register.

By the 1970s, Cleveland Union Terminal's steam concourse was a very different place from what it had been during the railroad's heyday. Before it would be reborn, it would first suffer more indignities. (Cleveland Press Collection of the Cleveland State University Libraries)

The bustle was gone from the once teeming CUT concourses. In the old steam concourse, two tennis courts replaced the benches which had once been filled by travelers awaiting departures on the 12 tracks below. Ugly fluorescent lighting fixtures replaced the grand old bronze chandeliers. Most of the stairways which had led down to track level were boarded over. The two that remained were used by automobile owners to get to and from their cars in the parking lot which had replaced the former coach yards behind the station. The popular English Oak dining room closed its doors in 1975, and the other concessions run by Harvey's, the national railroad station service chain, closed in 1977.

Paint chips regularly fell from the concourse ceilings, and missing chunks of plaster and water stains were graphic evidence of the neglect afflicting the once grand station. It was no longer the place where people would meet to start off a day or night on the town. CUT's remaining usefulness was as a walkway for rapid transit patrons and off-Square parkers.

By the late 1970s the steam concourse of the union terminal was usually empty, its glory days fading into memory. The sign directs people to the parking lot below, which formerly had been the track level for the facility. The mural pictured is now displayed in the Western Reserve Historical Society. *(Jack Muslovski photo, Jim Toman Collection)*

Although not much in the Public Square neighborhood represented progress, in 1972 the Square did get a bit brighter. Added to the Christmas lights in the Square that year was a flashing news sign on the Williamson Building. Stretching some 116 feet along its Euclid Avenue frontage and wrapping around another 92 feet on its Public Square side, the sign used 2,268 bulbs. It was reminiscent of the familiar electric sign in New York's Times Square. The sign began flashing its messages on December 18.

The May Company continued to be sensitive to the changes that were occurring in downtown retailing. In 1967 the store had its terra cotta frontage cleaned, the first phase in a major renovation. In 1968 the company installed modern new escalators, and in 1969 it unveiled a redesigned first floor selling space. And while May's downtown store was weathering the public's changing shopping habits better than had its three departed rivals, it too was facing thinner crowds of shoppers. Symbolic of that downward trend was May's closing all retail operations in its Ontario Street building. That happened on November 11, 1977. May's explained its action as a move to modernize its men's department, which for years had occupied the first floor of the Ontario store. The underlying reality, however, was that the giant store no longer needed all of its former retail space. Shopping had largely become a suburban mall phenomenon.

Perhaps the most shocking development on the Square was the financial collapse of the Hotel Cleveland enterprise. Facing increasingly difficult times, the Sheraton chain sold the hotel to a group of investors in 1975. The new ownership announced plans for a major renovation of the hotel, but it lacked the capital to carry them out. Troubles mounted, and in November 1976 the hotel went into receivership, and eventually was put up for bid in a sheriff's sale. A group of civic leaders, led by then Cleveland Browns' President Art Modell, raised

The southeast quadrant of the Square became a bit brighter in 1972 when the Williamson Building added a moving news sign above its second floor windows. The days for both the sign and the building, however, were numbered. *(Cleveland Press Collection of the Cleveland State University Libraries)*

Development moved nearer to the Square in the 1970s when the City and the County combined to build a new Justice Center on Ontario Street just one block north of the Square. *(Jim Toman photo)*

$18,000,000 to purchase and renovate the hotel. In the meantime, however, the hotel could not remain open for business. On August 1, 1977, its doors were closed to permit the renovation to take place. Just as the union station had outlived its early days of glory, so too the hotel, which had been built to accommodate the railroad traveling public, found its occupancy rate in steady decline. An airline ticketing office occupied a part of the railroad hotel's once grand lobby. Times indeed had changed.

The Lausche State Office Building at West Sixth Street and Superior Avenue opened in 1978. Original plans called for the building to be connected to Cleveland Union Terminal by means of an underground passage, but cost-cutting kept the connector from being built. *Last* by sculptor Tony Smith is in front of the building. *(Jim Toman photo)*

The 1970s did bring some developmental stirrings not too far off the Square. The huge Cleveland-Cuyahoga County Justice Center complex rose just one block north of the Square, between St. Clair and Lakeside avenues. The Justice Center was dedicated in September 1976. To the west of the Square, next to the main Post Office, the State of Ohio put up a new state office building. Named after former Cleveland mayor, Ohio governor, and U.S. Senator Frank J. Lausche, the state office complex was opened in November 1978. Development was moving closer to the Square than during the Erieview heyday, but the area immediately surrounding the central city green remained in stasis.

Downtown lost another attraction in 1976 when the 42nd floor observation deck of the Terminal Tower was closed to the public. In August of that year, an angry Ashby Leach invaded the executive offices of the Chessie System railroad on the Tower's 36th floor and held several company executives hostage to protest the company's hiring practices. Although the hostages were released unharmed nine hours later, the incident revealed a fundamental building security weakness.

The trip to the 42nd floor observation deck was not a one-elevator ride. Because of the way that the upper floors of the tower narrowed, ground floor elevators reached from lobby level only to the 32nd floor, where visitors had to transfer to a second set for the final 10-story climb. This transfer made monitoring the office tower's traffic difficult. To reduce the risk to tenants, the observation deck was closed, and a security checkpoint was established on the 32nd floor. For nearly 50 years, the Terminal Tower's observation deck had been a popular downtown attraction for young and old alike, for native Clevelanders as well as for tourists. Its new role would be as a private corporate conference room.

Two years later the Square neighborhood lost another attraction. For 70 years Shroeder's Books and News had been a fixture. Its location on the first floor of the Cuyahoga Building, at the East Roadway and Superior Avenue, and its broad range of greeting cards, newspapers, magazines, books, snacks, and tobacco products had made it a popular stop for both busy commuters and more leisurely shoppers. When Schroeder's closed in April 1979, the Square lost one of its most appealing presences.

In its slumber, Public Square continued to be an honest mirror of the city's ebbing vitality. Then in 1976 the Square itself became the catalyst for energizing the efforts to restore downtown as a people place. In that year the Garden Club of Cleveland assumed leadership of a determined effort to reinvigorate the central green. It had been 46 years since the last total makeover of the Square had taken place, and though there had been periodic shrub and tree replacements during that stretch of time, as well as some suggestions for a total renovation, it was not until the Garden Club took the reins that any substantive redesign took place.

Other proposals had come and gone. In 1958 a proposal had been made to rename Cleveland's central green Cleveland International Square. The concept was tied into the vision that the soon-to-open St. Lawrence Seaway would bring new international trade and vigor to the city. The plan called for the Square to be recessed below street level and for both Superior Avenue and Ontario Street to end at the perimeter road that would surround a sunken central plaza. A 1962 plan called for just the opposite. It suggested elevating the Square so that Superior Avenue could be tunneled beneath it. Ontario Street would be truncated at the perimeter roadway, and the Square itself would be reconfigured into a terraced central plaza. In 1975 a plan by urban designer Lawrence Halprin also suggested that Superior Avenue be tunneled under the Square and that Ontario Street end at the Square's perimeter. He also suggested that a vintage streetcar line operate from Public Square to Playhouse Square along a Euclid Avenue which would be translated into a pedestrian/transit mall. All of these concepts would have ended the Square's configuration into four separate quadrants. Nothing came of them.

A recurring suggestion from planners has been to close off the streets which divide the Square into four separate quadrants. In the 1960s one such idea Superior Avenue running beneath an elevated Square and Ontario Street truncated at the Square's outer roadways. (*Cleveland* Press *Collection of the Cleveland State University Libraries*)

One plan that would have affected the Public Square landscape came closer to fruition. In 1976 Cleveland Mayor Ralph Perk, acting in consort with the Greater Cleveland Regional Transit Authority (RTA), had applied for a federal Department of Transportation demonstration grant to build an elevated rail line. Dubbed a people-mover, the line would have operated in a loop running from Public Square to Playhouse Square to Erieview at East 12th and Lakeside Avenue, and then back to Ontario Street and the Square. The mayor and RTA saw the proposal as giving downtown Cleveland the transit distribution system that had been lost when the county commissioners decided against the subway plan. Cleveland's application was one of four accepted by the federal agency, but Cleveland's next mayor, Dennis Kucinich, decided to turn down the grant. While his action was bitterly criticized by Cleveland City Council members, his decision ultimately spared Public Square the indignity of a forest of concrete support pillars and a cumbersome overhead guideway, as well as other complications (if events in Detroit, which accepted the plan, are any indicator).

In 1976 the Garden Club's Public Square initiative found a more fertile ground. Its $200,000 in seed money together with another $100,000 grant from the Cleveland Foundation permitted serious planning to get underway. The firm of Sasaki Associates of Watertown, Massachusetts, was commissioned to undertake the design work, and its plan was unveiled on September 27, 1977. The Sasaki concept called for keeping the Square's four quadrants but redesigning the three that were under the jurisdiction of the City of Cleveland while also modifying the streetscape of Superior Avenue and Ontario Street.

In the early 1970s, before Public Square would again become the focus of downtown redevelopment, the area looked tired. In 1976 planners began to tackle the issue of how the Square could again become an inviting and interesting public space. *(Cleveland* Press *Collection of the Cleveland State University Libraries)*

The Sasaki plan drew broad critical support and was approved by Cleveland City Council, which then applied for federal economic development grants to fund the makeover. The official start of the project took place on October 20, 1977, when HRH Charles, Prince of Wales, then visiting Cleveland, planted a ceremonial first tree on the northeast quadrant, the first of the three quadrants to undergo redesign. His tree was soon relocated so that work could begin on the complete reconstruction of the quadrant. The renovation of the Square would continue for another nine years. The front room of the city was about to get its long overdue facelift.

Even though physical changes to the Square and in the buildings that enfolded it had been few during this time period, and though downtown itself had lost its position as a shopping and entertainment center, Public Square continued to serve as the ceremonial center of the city, and as in decades past, many events of political and social significance took place there.

Not only has Public Square been a prime location for local events and leaders, it has also been a favorite location for U.S. presidents on the campaign trail. In 1952 President Harry S. Truman came to Cleveland to speak on behalf of the Democratic candidate for president, Adlai Stevenson. A huge partisan crowd in the Square, carrying "Give 'em Hell, Harry" placards, cheered the speech he delivered from a platform in front of the Terminal Tower. In 1956 Truman's Republican successor Dwight D. Eisenhower came to Cleveland as part of his drive for a second term. He also used Public Square as the venue for his campaign rhetoric.

A huge crowd gathered to hear President Harry S. Truman speak on behalf of Adlai Stevenson in October 1952. As the sign in the lower right hand corner indicates, the partisan crowd expected Truman to "give 'em hell." (Cleveland Press Collection of the Cleveland State University Libraries)

Presidents were not the only celebrities to visit Public Square. Here General Douglas A. MacArthur's car is about to turn onto Euclid Avenue in September 1951. He was in Cleveland just five months after he was relieved of his duties by President Truman. Truman's action probably only enhanced the general's popularity, as is evident by the sizable crowd which cheered him on. *(Cleveland Press Collection of the Cleveland State University Libraries)*

In 1960 both presidential candidates, John F. Kennedy and Richard M. Nixon, had their motorcades pass through Public Square. On September 27 Kennedy was on his way to Euclid Beach Park where he was the key speaker at the Cuyahoga County Democratic Party steer roast. An estimated 120,000 attended the affair there. Vice President Nixon's plane arrived at Burke Lakefront Airport on October 6, and his motorcade made its way to Public Square and the Sheraton Cleveland Hotel. Police estimated that 150,000 lined the route and the Square to cheer his arrival. He later spoke to a crowd of 18,500 in a joint Public Hall/Music Hall rally.

President Kennedy returned to Cleveland on October 19, 1962, for a Democratic rally in Public Square in support of that year's congressional campaign. The mid-day speech from a platform in front of the Terminal Tower only lasted 8½ minutes, but a crowd variously estimated at between 40,000-100,000 cheered on the popular president's rhetoric.

On June 7, 1964, President Lyndon B. Johnson spoke at a Public Square rally, and then he followed his speech with a Square walkabout, a people-pleasing tactic made popular by HM Queen Elizabeth II. Johnson also returned to downtown Cleveland that fall for a fundraising dinner in Public Hall.

Richard Nixon's next campaign for the presidency brought him to Cleveland once again. In June 1968 he addressed the crowd from a booth in front of the Terminal Tower. President Gerald Ford was a frequent visitor to the city, but his visits tended to focus on stumping in the neighborhoods.

Public Square continued to serve not only as the place where aspiring political leaders rallied the voters, but it also remained the place where Clevelanders memorialized their fallen leaders. No services, however, were held on the Square for President Kennedy in November 1963. On the day of his funeral in Washington, D.C., downtown Cleveland was silent and empty. The stores were closed, and most Greater Clevelanders were either attending services in their neighborhood churches, or they were glued to their television sets to watch the ceremonies in the nation's capital.

Following the assassination of Martin Luther King, Jr., in 1968, however, Public Square once again was the venue for people to show respect and share their grief. Senator Robert F. Kennedy, then on campaign for the 1968 Democratic presidential nomination, was in Cleveland to get local support for his candidacy. When he learned of King's death in Memphis, he canceled his political plans, and instead delivered a eulogy at an Old Stone Church memorial service. The church could not hold the throng that came for the service, and it overflowed out onto Public Square.

But as the heart of the city, Public Square necessarily had to draw the common folk as well as the exalted. And there has been nothing which has done that better than parades. Some downtown parades began on the Mall. Most began on Euclid Avenue east of Playhouse Square. All of them, however, wended their way through Public Square where the largest crowds gathered to watch.

As custom had come to dictate, the three stars of the parade season signaled St. Patrick's Day, Memorial Day, and the Christmas season, the latter parade usually held on the weekend following Thanksgiving Day.

Downtown's Memorial Day ceremonies tend to draw the smallest crowds, competing as they do with similar celebrations held in all the suburbs. Typical of the downtown event was the Memorial Day

Holiday decorations and the Christmas parade were major events during the 1950s. Here downtown workers enjoy the lights as they await their transit trip home. *(Cleveland* Press *Collection of the Cleveland State University Libraries)*

service of 1971, the 103rd annual commemoration of those fallen in service to the nation. The 1971 services paid particular tribute to the 25 Clevelanders who had died in the Vietnam struggle during the previous twelve months. At noon dignitaries, accompanied by a color guard, firing squad, and a contingent of Gold Star mothers, laid wreaths in the Square. A total of about 300 people attended the service. Later that afternoon the crowd swelled to about 10,000 for the parade which began at the War Memorial Fountain on the Mall, and then made its way through Public Square and on to East Ninth Street.

St. Patrick's Day parades, by nature, were both more festive and better attended. The 1979 parade, the 112th such event, was typical. For the occasion, city work crews applied green paint over the yellow street dividing lines marking the parade route from the Cleveland State University campus through Public Square and then past a reviewing stand on Superior Avenue.

An enthusiastic crowd of some 230,000 onlookers, most sporting something green, cheered on the 106 units in the parade.

One of the largest crowds in the history of Public Square gathered on April 27, 1952, to witness a "Parade of Progress," held to mark the end of streetcar service on Euclid Avenue. These people await the cavalcade of vehicles which would turn from Euclid Avenue. *(Cleveland Transit System photo, Blaine Hays Collection)*

For many years the Christmas parade was the most popular marching event. On November 26, 1955, police estimated the downtown crowd lining Euclid Avenue from East 18th Street to the Square at over 300,000. The parade units gathered in a large parking lot, where Cleveland State University's main buildings are now located. Parade headquarters were in the old Hotel Amsterdam on Euclid Avenue and East 22nd Street (where Viking Hall stands today). The parade route was lined several deep all the way to and through the Square and onto Superior Avenue. As had become the custom, Santa Claus waved to the crowds from the last float in the parade.

The 1955 Christmas Parade seems to share the downtown crowd record with another parade which took place on April 27, 1952. Labeled the Parade of Progress, that event marked the end of streetcar operation on Euclid Avenue. To mark the historic occasion (streetcars, and horse cars before them, had run on Euclid since 1859) the parade represented a cavalcade of transport progress. A long line of transit vehicles, stretching all the way east to East 30th Street and other transport units filling the East 18th-21st Street parking lot made up the parade which began at East 18th Street. All the vehicles were accompanied by people in period costume. Typical entries included an ox cart, riders on horseback, horse-drawn carriages, horse-drawn streetcars, antique fire engines, steam-, electric, and gasoline-powered automobiles, vintage and modern electric streetcars, and the newest diesel buses. As with the Christmas parade, police estimated the crowd at over 300,000.

Begun in the 1970s, Friday "Parties in the Park" were begun to boost downtown by encouraging workers to stay downtown after work. The parties alternated among downtown's various public spaces. This one drew thousands to the Square. *(Cleveland* Press *Collection of the Cleveland State University Libraries)*

Protest was another recurring feature of the era on Public Square. Probably the defining historical event for the 1960-1970s was the war in Vietnam, an event which polarized the nation. Locally, war protesters took full advantage of the free speech tradition on the Square to challenge the government's southeast Asia policies. Demonstrators used all four quadrants of the Square at various times in their 1964-1974 anti-war campaign. Favorite spots, however, were on the northeast quadrant to target the adjacent Federal Building, on the southeast quadrant by the monument to an even bloodier war, and on the northeast quadrant by Tom Johnson's free speech rostrum. Typical of the events on the northeast quadrant were a 1966 "Speak Out" against the war, a 1968 "Litany of Penitence" for war excesses, and a 1971 peace rally. The anti-war demonstrations were many and varied, and throughout the decade of protest they were a regular feature on the Public Square scene.

The hotel on the Square was completely renovated in 1978, reopening as Stouffer's Inn on the Square (now the Renaissance Cleveland Hotel). *(Stouffer Corporation photo, Jim Toman Collection).*

As the 1970s came to an end, a Clevelander's vision of what the final two decades of the century would bring to the Square and to the city was understandably murky. On September 22, 1978, the old Hotel Cleveland reopened its doors as Stouffer's Inn on the Square. The splendidly restored building was certainly a sign of hope for downtown's future. But just two months later, on December 15, as a result of the continued feuding between the city's youthful Mayor Dennis Kucinich on one side and the City Council and the city's corporate leadership on the other, the City of Cleveland found itself in financial default. The event shocked the community, and many feared that the city's future looked bleak indeed. Then just a few months later, Clevelanders overwhelmingly approved an increase in the city's income tax rate. They had signaled their willingness to do their part to help the city recover. But would it be enough?

Whither downtown, whither Public Square, whither the city itself? Would the city find renewed resolve to solve its problems, or was it doomed to continuing decline? As the last days of the 1970s waned, the answers to those questions were by no means clear.

They would, however, be answered in the next two decades, and as had been true before, the future of the city and of the venerable Square at its heart would unfold in parallel. The final chapter in the century's saga was about to be written.

A Resurgence
1980 - 1999

As the 1970s expired under a sluggish national economy and a host of other domestic and international problems, Cleveland experienced the same malaise that seemed to seep through the nation's fiber. In Cleveland, however, which had become a national joke for several infamous incidents that made national headlines, the situation seemed even worse. A series of crises, ranging from a heavily polluted river that caught fire to the City's fiscal default, the first by any major city in the history of the U.S., shook Cleveland's leadership and residents' confidence in the town. Declining population figures, deteriorating downtown areas, and the painfully slow development of urban planning projects combined to keep the Greater Cleveland area seemingly stagnant.

In 1980, 573,822 people called the city of Cleveland their home. That number was a startling drop of 30.8% from the 1970 U.S. census numbers. As a result, Cleveland slipped from the tenth largest city in the nation to the 18th. The county, too, had lost population, but the city's share of it continued its decrease to only 38% of the Cuyahoga total. While the number of residents in the Greater Cleveland metropolitan area continued to grow, they were living at distances farther from the city's center than ever before. For people to navigate these distances to come downtown, they had to have compelling reason.

As the 1980s opened, the signals about downtown were mostly discouraging. Several familiar downtown enterprises entered the history books. On May 1, 1980, the Cleveland Plaza hotel (formerly the Statler and Statler-Hilton) closed. It would be converted to office use. One day later, on May 2, the Hippodrome Theater, the last surviving Euclid Avenue movie palace, screened its last film. The building was torn down for a parking garage. The city was then further impacted by a nationwide recession which doomed two more downtown venerable institutions.

On January 27, 1982, the Halle Brothers department store on Playhouse Square turned off its lights for good, the fourth of the city's one-time-six downtown department stores to close. Since 1970 the store had been owned by the Marshall Field Company of Chicago, but the store's reputation for quality and service, which had been firmly established under the guidance of Cleveland's Halle family, had remained strong. Despite its reputation, however, sales lagged through the 1970s, and in November 1981 the store was sold once again, this time to a Columbus, Ohio, operator. While the sale was accompanied by confident words about the store's future, just two months later, its closing was announced.

Only five months later, on June 17, 1982, another shock rippled through the city as Joseph Cole, owner of the Cleveland *Press*, the city's afternoon daily for 104 years, announced it would cease publication effective that day. The loss of these hallowed Cleveland institutions chilled whatever optimism Clevelanders were trying to muster in the post-default years. Downtown retailing suffered yet another blow in 1984 when the S. S. Kresge Company announced that it would close its large Public Square store, which occupied the easternmost section of the May Company building. Though the store had remained modestly profitable, company officials were interested in focusing their attention on their new suburban K-Mart division. After 75 years on the Square, Kresge's closed its doors for the last time on December 29, 1984.

Downtown's two remaining department stores were also facing difficult times. The May Company and the Higbee Company buildings had been built at a time when every square foot of retail space was important, but by the 1980s the size of the stores had become a detriment rather than an advantage. In the early 1980s Higbee's leased two of its upper floors to Women's Federal Savings and Loan and to Sohio for office space. Two of May's upper floors were being used by Society National Bank, and another by Cardinal Federal Savings and Loan. Lease income had become a critical supplement to sales volume for the two retailers.

Amid the gloom of downtown's declining retail environment, there were a few developments of a brighter nature. Perhaps fittingly, these emanated from the city's most revered landmark, the Terminal Tower complex. On July 13, 1981, the Public Square neighborhood became a bit brighter when U.S. Realty Investments, then the owner of the Terminal Tower, flipped the switch to bathe the building's night-time profile in a golden glow. Then, under the auspices of the Cleveland Convention and Visitors' Bureau, the public once again gained access to the structure's 42nd floor observation deck. Although at first open only on weekends and during the summer and the Christmas shopping season, the deck's reopening allowed a new group of Clevelanders the opportunity to enjoy what had been a traditional downtown experience for generations. In April 1984, the deck's visiting hours were extended to weekends all year long. Since then some 10,000-15,000 people yearly have taken advantage of it.

The nearly vacant concourses in the Union Terminal were also showing new signs of life, as the eastern traction concourse was converted into a fast food court and new shops opened in the ticket lobby area of the steam concourse. In 1983, the skylight in the steam concourse, which had been covered over since the war years, was restored, and natural light once again flooded the formerly dreary waiting area. These changes could perhaps have been understood as signals that attention was again being focused on the city's hub. They were certainly precursors of the much more dynamic changes that would soon transform the Public Square neighborhood.

In 1982 the Terminal Tower received a lighting makeover. It was the first time that the Tower was bathed from top to bottom in an amber glow. The snowy conditions give the Tower an unusual aura. *(Cleveland* **Press** *Collection of the Cleveland State University Libraries)*

So although the last two decades of the century opened with mixed signals, what would emerge during them would be remarkable, given the decades of inertia which had characterized the Square's immediate vicinity. As the relationship between City officials, led by Mayor George Voinovich and City Council President George Forbes, and area businesses began to improve in the early 1980s, Clevelanders once again were able to read in the newspapers about development plans. Over the remaining years of the century, the town's hub would witness many exciting changes that would dramatically alter the landscape and the skyline of the city.

The changes to the Public Square neighborhood actually began on the city green itself. The first phase of the Public Square makeover plan that had begun in fall 1978 was completed only months before Clevelanders welcomed the 1980s. The renovation began when the City erected an unattractive wooden fence on the perimeter of the Square's northeast quadrant (so that pedestrians would not walk into the construction site), but behind the barricade the town green had begun to take on a fresh new look. While the renovation of the entire Square would not be completed until 1986, many Clevelanders viewed the ongoing facelift as a portent of better times.

Work then moved over to the northwest quadrant. A principal piece in the redesign for the northern quadrants (which are slightly larger than the southern two) involved reducing the width of the east-west perimeter roads by 26 feet and those on the north-south axis by six feet. On the northeast quadrant, workers installed a new fountain, benches, lighting, and bus shelters at a cost of $2.7 million in federal, state, and local funds. They also added new shrubbery and trees and installed brick walkways along the perimeter.

On the northwest quadrant local and state funds totaling $1 million also helped beautify the grass, trees, and walkways. The changes there also included moving the Tom L. Johnson statue from the center of the quadrant to its northern edge, slightly elevating the central green area, and adding brick pavers to the surrounding walkways. The revered free speech rostrum, long the focal point of advocates and dissidents alike, disappeared with the renovations.

The southeast quadrant did not go without improvements, either. While the City had no responsibility for that quadrant, in 1985 the County, which was in charge of that quadrant, announced its own plans to spruce up that part of the downtown park. Sasaki & Associates were again the designers. The County had already renovated the famous Soldiers and Sailors Monument itself. In this phase, it spent an additional $40,000 to rework the landscaping and walkways around the Civil War memorial.

The greatest outlay of funds, though, was reserved for the southwest quadrant, also referred to as the Terminal quadrant. In 1983, the state provided $4 million in grant moneys so that the City could install a central recessed plaza, paved in dark brick, which was to be bordered on several sides by overlooks to accommodate speeches and ceremonies. Perhaps reflecting the earlier presence of a waterfall on that quadrant, workers installed a multi-layered cascading fountain along the area's northern edge. The Moses Cleaveland statue was repositioned from the center to the western edge of the central plaza. In addition, workers put double rows of shade trees along Ontario Street and Superior Avenue, and the entire quadrant was further enhanced by ornamental stone work. In 1986 workers completed the last step of the project with the installation of historic lighting fixtures. In the end, the final price tag for the physical renovation of the entire Public Square was $12 million.

Clevelanders greeted the physical facelift of the park with a rededication ceremony on July 22, 1986. Representatives from the State, the City, and the Garden Club activated the pumps to the new fountain on the southwest quadrant as they spoke of the town hub as another example of "public and private commitment to the Cleveland comeback." The ceremony also marked the 150th anniversary of the City's incorporation.

These scenes from the Terminal Tower show the three quadrants of Public Square that were completely renovated by 1986 (top northeast; middle, northwest; bottom, southwest). *(Greg Deegan photos)*

While local officials and groups charged ahead to make the Square more pedestrian-friendly and park-like, residents in early 1981 began to hear rumors of a more massive project that might take shape on Public Square. In November the Standard Oil Company of Ohio (now BP Amoco) confirmed the rumors. Corporation officials announced that they had decided to erect a new headquarters building between Euclid and Superior avenues overlooking the Square's southeast quadrant.

The Standard Oil Company had a long and gloried history in Cleveland. Made an international player in the oil industry by John D. Rockefeller in the late 19th and early 20th centuries, the corporation helped propel Cleveland's rise to prominence as a center of manufacturing and industry at a time when the nation's economic structure was burgeoning. By the late 1970s, the company was the city's largest corporation, but some observers thought they perceived ominous signs about Sohio's future in Cleveland.

Headquartered in the Midland Building, behind the Terminal Tower, but with offices spread among eight different downtown buildings, Sohio had been cramped for office space for some time. In 1977, officials had announced they would move into a 22-story tower to be built above the old railroad coach yards just south of Huron Road. Then in 1978 the corporation canceled those plans, explaining that its assets were needed to develop the Alaskan pipeline.

Many observers took the news as a sign that Standard Oil was planning to leave Cleveland. Those rumors persisted until February 1981 when word leaked that company officials were looking into sites on Public Square for a new building. When Sohio officials finally revealed their plans, they called for a 46-story, $200 million tower ($328 million in 1999 dollars) with an atrium overlooking the northeast quadrant of the

Square (directly across Euclid Avenue from where the company's first offices had been located 111 years earlier). The price tag for the project would make it the most expensive in Cleveland construction history at the time.

To make room for the proposed structure, the Cuyahoga and Williamson buildings, which had overlooked the Square since the start of the 20th century, had to be removed along with other buildings east of those edifices. Many decried the loss of the venerable buildings. The 82-year old Cuyahoga Building, designed by architect Daniel H. Burnham, was Cleveland's first steel-framed building and had been listed on the National Register of Historic Places since 1974. It also once housed the headquarters of the Cleveland Baseball Club. In those days, whenever the team was playing at home, the club would position a huge baseball at the top of the flagpole on the roof, easily visible to pedestrians in the Square. The 16-story Williamson Building, at the time of its construction in 1900, had been the tallest in

the city. Gone too to make room for the Sohio Building would be other pieces of downtown and Public Square history: the Mall Theatre, Mills Restaurant, Rosenblum's clothing store, and the main offices of financial institutions such as Women's Federal and Cardinal Federal Savings and Loan. While some fretted over the loss to the city's architectural and cultural heritage, many others greeted the proposed plans with anticipation and excitement. Area preservationists did celebrate a minor victory. They were able to save the main entrance archway to the Cuyahoga Building, which was subsequently incorporated into the eastern wall of the Western Reserve Historical Society's new library building in University Circle.

In October 1982 Baltimore-based Controlled Demolition, Inc. oversaw the imploding of the Cuyahoga and Williamson structures. Although the implosion itself proceeded without problems, there was a scare shortly

In order to make way for the new Standard Oil development on the Square, the venerable Cuyahoga and Williamson buildings were imploded. The structures were wiped from the Public Square neighborhood in just under 10 seconds. *(Standard Oil Company photo, Jim Toman Collection)*

before the event. Two days prior to the planned implosion, the supports for the sidewalk beneath the northwest corner of the Cuyahoga Building mysteriously collapsed, bringing down with them the corner section of the structure's first six floors. The structural integrity of the building was unaffected and nobody was hurt, but it did make safety officials cordon off the area earlier than they had anticipated. On Sunday morning, October 3, approximately 6,000 onlookers witnessed the implosion firsthand. The buildings took less than ten seconds to fall. A dust cloud about seven stories high rose from the rubble, showering the onlookers with a fine gray powder.

Groundbreaking ceremonies for the new tower took place in December 1982. Then workers got busy on the foundation. They drilled caissons to 240 feet below the surface to assure a stable footing for the massive weight that would rise on them. They were the deepest caissons in North America. Atop the foundation, a total load of 20,000 tons of structural steel was erected, the last beam fitted into place in June 1984. Then the building's granite skin, in shades of red and mahogany, was attached. More than 4000 panels were required to cover the tower. Bronze-tinted windows finished the exterior detailing on three sides of the building, while the northern exposure received clear glass.

In April 1984 construction on the Sohio Building is well underway. Work is just beginning on the frame of the atrium which will adjoin the Square's southeast quadrant. *(Jim Toman photo)*

The new skyscraper, designed by Hellmuth, Obata & Kassabaum (HOK) of St. Louis, rose 45 stories and reached 653.9 feet above Public Square. While the architects had of course taken into account the needs of the corporation, they were also sensitive to the site the tower would occupy on the city's central green. To have the new Standard Oil Building complement Public Square, designers proposed that an atrium of eight stories connect the building to its Public Square frontage. The atrium contained 110,000 square feet, 40,000 devoted to retail, 34,000 to open space, and the remainder for offices. It was intended as a public place which would have, besides office and commercial areas, a great deal of open space.

The plans were also sensitive to the Terminal Tower. The new tower was kept 55 feet shorter than the Square's venerable guardian, apparently as a sign of respect for the city's landmark building. At the urging of the City Planning Commission, HOK also decided to trim the upper stories with four setbacks, a feature which was intended stylistically to match the new building's upper floors with those of the Tower. And lastly, the walls of the office tower facing the downtown park were hinged inward toward the center. This tended to downplay the considerable bulk of the structure, again showing sensitivity to the Terminal's slender profile, while at the same time keeping each of the building's sides perpendicular to Euclid and Superior avenues.

When the Standard Oil Building was completed in 1985, it offered 1.2 million square feet of office space, its total surpassing that of all other high rises and actually doubling the available space in the Terminal Tower. The Sohio total also far exceeded that of the city's largest privately owned office building, the Huntington Building, which had 879,000 square feet of office space. The structure was dedicated on April 19, 1986. Its name was changed to the BP America Building on May 12, 1989, when British Petroleum bought Sohio.

Across the Square from the Sohio Building, the venerable Society for Savings building housed an ever-growing corporation. As the Society Corporation expanded in the early 1970s into a statewide banking power, the old, cramped building at 127 Public Square that had served since 1890 as the organization's headquarters was no longer able to meet the institution's needs. In September 1980, Society Corporation, crunched for space, found a temporary

The completed Standard Oil Building dwarfed all of its neighbors but one. The structure was kept 55 feet shorter than the Terminal as a sign of respect to the older building's historic landmark status. *(Jim Toman photo)*

In 1986 the Society for Savings building had outlived its usefulness- -but not its significance.
Its future played a key piece in plans for the Square's next major development. *(Jim Toman photo)*

solution in the abandoned Ontario Building of the May Company. The bank then purchased the structure and at the same time leased the sixth floor of the May Company's main building for additional space.

Then Society Corporation grew even larger. In January 1985 the company announced its agreement to acquire Centran Corporation, parent organization of Cleveland's Central National Bank. The move made Society one of Ohio's largest banks and hastened its need for more office space. In 1986 Society reluctantly moved its headquarters from its historic building on the town green to the former headquarters of Central National Bank (now the McDonald & Company Building) at the corner of East Ninth Street and Superior Avenue. But the fit there was tight, too, and officials soon realized that the move was a temporary solution.

Part of the reality of downtown Cleveland during this time period was the diminishing number of hotel rooms. A 1987 City-sponsored study revealed that since 1959 the downtown area had lost 60% of its hotel rooms. As the City and the Convention and Visitors Bureau of Greater Cleveland joined in 1983 to renovate the Cleveland Convention Center on Mall B, local business and civic leaders realized that in order to attract convention business to the new state-of-the-art facility, the city had to stop the downtown drainage of hotel rooms.

So it made sense in 1986, with the old Society for Savings Building standing empty and its future uncertain, that some observers speculated that the Burnham and Root landmark might be converted into much needed hotel space. These proponents felt that a restored light court surrounded by hotel rooms would make an ideal guest facility. Others suggested simply razing the old building and starting from scratch. A study sponsored by Society officials determined that the building could not be converted into suitable hotel space. The study, done by Galbreath Company of Columbus, did suggest,

The Jacobs brothers' interest in downtown development was made clear when construction got underway on the Galleria--a shopping mall in Erieview. The scene is from March 1987.
(Jim Toman photo)

however, that a combination hotel/office tower would be an effective use of the site.

By the end of 1986, Society Corporation officials determined they would try to orchestrate the development of the Public Square site. In order to carry out such a task, Society purchased the Mall Building at East Second Street and St. Clair Avenue, extending its control to three quarters of the block (the Brotherhood of Locomotive Engineers Building remained in the union's hands). Principals from the bank approached three developers from outside Cleveland and asked each to work on a plan for a hotel/office building combination in which Society would be the anchor tenant. While Society looked elsewhere for plans, a local group emerged with its own ideas for developing the property.

The Jacobs, Visconsi & Jacobs Company, later renamed The Richard and David Jacobs Group in 1991 and now The Richard Jacobs Group, had purchased the Erieview Tower and had gained local notice for developing the attached Galleria at Erieview shopping mall. The Galleria project, begun in 1985 and opened in 1987, was the first significant investment in new downtown retail space since construction of the Bond's store on Euclid Avenue and East Ninth Street 40 years earlier. Fresh from their first downtown Cleveland venture, the Jacobs interests were intrigued by the possibilities that the Public Square site offered, and so they submitted a proposal.

At about the same time, preservationist groups like the Cleveland Restoration Society and the Cleveland Chapter of the American Institute of Architects began to lobby for the preservation of the historic Burnham and Root building. Images of the recently imploded Cuyahoga Building still made some observers wary of the price further downtown development might exact from the city's architectural heritage. The Society for Savings Building, for instance, had landmark status; it was placed upon the National Register on November 7, 1976. Eric Johannesen, noted Cleveland preservationist for the Western Reserve Historical Society, had asserted in a local story that Cleveland could not do without the building, partly because Public Square was so important an urban space in Cleveland.

Responding to these concerns, Society officials made clear that preservation of its old headquarters had been made a prerequisite for any acceptable development proposal. The Jacobs plan for the site included a commitment to the preservation of 127 Public Square building as well as for a convention-sized hotel, two aspects of their plan that eventually earned them the right to develop the site.

When plans were announced for the new Society Center development, this computer-generated image gave Clevelanders a sense of what the new tower would look like on Public Square. Before construction began, the Society Tower underwent minor alterations from this model. *(Cesar Pelli & Associates)*

As the details of the proposed renovation and building began to emerge, area residents learned that the Jacobs interests planned a $30 million rehabilitation of the Burnham and Root building as well as the construction of a 50-story connecting tower. Although not yet settled at the time, the scope of the development would include a large parking facility beneath Mall A, the total rehabilitation of that portion of the Mall, as well as the site occupied by the Brotherhood of Locomotive Engineers' Building on St. Clair Avenue and Ontario Street. While preservationists hoped that this structure could also be rehabilitated, studies suggested such a venture would be too costly for any developer to consider seriously.

What intrigued Clevelanders the most, however, was the rumor that the new tower would edge out the Terminal Tower, its soon-to-be neighbor across the town green, as the city's tallest structure. On December 4, 1987, the City Planning Commission voted unanimously to change the height restriction on the old Chamber of Commerce site from 250 to 900 feet. The change gave substance to the rumors which promised to alter dramatically the look and feel of Public Square and its environs.

The City's willingness to change the height restriction was particularly meaningful to local skyline watchers. When plans for the Sohio Building were emerging just eight years before, the height of the Terminal Tower seemed then to have been sacrosanct. It was not to be challenged by developers. But times had changed. Whereas tradition had governed the thinking during the Sohio development, excitement about the ongoing renaissance of the city had come to the planning forefront. The city needed new symbols to mark its comeback.

On January 26, 1988, at a news conference in the old Society for Savings Building on the Square, the plans for the new office tower were finally revealed. Those present included representatives from The Richard and David Jacobs Group, Society Corporation officials, city and county leaders, and New Haven, Connecticut, architect, Cesar Pelli. Pelli was the former dean of the Yale School of Architecture, and he had to his credit the 739-foot World Financial Center in New York as well as the pyramidal Cleveland Clinic Crile Building, which had opened three years earlier to favorable reviews.

Pelli had much to say about the proposed tower and its place on Public Square. According to him, a good architect respects that which is already in place. In this case, he said he was trying to design the new tower with the Burnham and Root Building foremost in his mind. To allow the old building to retain its dignity and prominence on the Square and in local history, the new tower was to be situated a few feet farther back from the town green. The proposed building would also have its first setback at the old Society for Savings' roof line, a feature intended to prevent the soaring new structure from overwhelming its much smaller neighbor. Finally, the connection between the two buildings would be set back from their fronts so that it would appear that the two buildings retained their separate identities.

Pelli also acknowledged that the new tower had to be a good neighbor to the Sohio Building and to the Terminal Tower. Like the Terminal, the new building was designed as a New York-style skyscraper--one that was essentially vertical, slender in profile, and pyramidal at the top. It would be designed to exude the feel of a classic American skyscraper of the 1930s. Though considerably taller than its neighbor across the Square, its narrow face (the side facing the Terminal was to be markedly narrower than the east/west sides) was meant to prevent it from overwhelming the venerable landmark.

The importance of Public Square, the city's most revered space, also played a vital role in Pelli's conception for the new complex. Pelli found the Cleveland skyline intriguing, dominated as it was by a single building, the Terminal Tower. Cleveland had been one of only a few U.S. cities with that distinctive profile. So it was that when the Sohio Building, which nearly rivaled the Terminal, was erected along the southeast quadrant of the city's hub, it helped to accentuate the Square. With the addition of the new Society Tower, three of the four quadrants would be bordered by soaring towers.

Work is under way on the Society Center project in November 1989. The scene looks south from St. Clair Avenue.   *(Jim Toman photo)*

Society Tower is nearly half grown in summer 1990. The view is from Euclid Avenue. The Federal Court House is at the right.   *(Jim Toman photo)*

They would combine to emphasize the centrality of Public Square in the civic life of Cleveland (and creating, according to Pelli, an enclosed area around the Square that gave the feel of an "outdoor living room"). As Pelli said, the Society project would "draw the center of gravity to where it belongs--Public Square."

Beyond the impressive physical addition it would bring to the town green, the Society Tower also marked the bank's commitment to the downtown area and to its home city. One company official proclaimed that the structure would be a "symbol of the renaissance and recovery of Cleveland, as one of the most important centers on the Great Lakes." Although one building does not a city make, it did seem to symbolize a reawakened civic vitality.

That one building soon spawned further development when in July 1988 the Jacobs Group secured ownership of the Engineers' Building. Plans called for the demolition of the old union headquarters and its replacement by a convention-sized Marriott Hotel and banquet facility. The Jacobs firm also gained responsibility for carrying out construction of the large parking garage to be built below Mall A. Previous plans for the garage had raised much concern about how the downtown's other green would be treated. The Jacobs Group committed itself to preserving the essential character of the Mall segment and of restoring its centerpiece, the War Memorial Fountain.

By the time actual construction started, Pelli had refined his original designs. Most notably, the tower had been slimmed down and had grown a notch or two. The final design called for a 57-story tower--up from the original 54 floors--at just over 888 feet, with a spire reaching 948 feet.

On October 17, 1988, officials met in the old Society for Savings Building parking lot. Because the surface lot was actually the roof of an underground parking level, dignitaries had to abandon the traditional groundbreaking shovel for a rope that was attached to a section of the wall that enclosed the parking space. At the designated moment, the assembled representatives gave a tug, and the old wall fell, helped by a nudge from a front-end loader stationed just behind it.

Excavation on the site began April 18, 1989. Altogether, 200,000 cubic yards of material were removed for the foundation. Once again, the caisson method was used to anchor the structure, some of the caissons burrowing 215 feet below ground level. Structural steelwork was underway by November, and 11 months later, on October 30, 1990,

The Terminal Tower's shadow grows shorter as the Society Tower across the Square rises ever higher. The scene also shows construction on the Society project's adjacent Marriott Hotel component. *(Jim Toman photo)*

When completed in 1991, the Society Tower reached higher than any other structure in Cleveland, taking that distinction from the Terminal Tower, which had been the city's tallest for a little more than 53 years. *(Greg Deegan photo)*

the framework surpassed the Terminal's height, ending that building's long reign as the city's tallest building. At the same time work was underway on the renovation of the original building, whose entire interior frame was removed and replaced by new floor plates capable of carrying the extra weight that modern business equipment required. The renovation, however, did not intrude on the landmark's elegant banking lobby. Rather than renovation, that space was treated to a thorough restoration.

Cleveland's newest building reached its ultimate height on May 14, 1991, when a crane positioned a 68-foot stainless steel spire to the top of the tower. The tip of the spire reached 948.7 feet above Public Square, and stood 175 feet higher than the flagpole atop the Terminal Tower.

On November 25, 1991, two-and-a-half years after construction had begun, the almost finished Society Tower saw its first tenant, the Deloitte & Touch accounting firm, move in. The main tenant, Society Corporation, followed suit in May 1992. The Marriott Hotel had its grand opening on November 22, 1991.

The completed project drew rave reviews. The old Burnham and Root building had been saved and restored, the city had gained a major new hotel, Mall A had been transfigured and its Fountain of Eternal Life (the War Memorial Fountain) centerpiece gleamingly restored, a large new underground parking garage with space for 982 vehicles had been opened beneath it, and the city's central park had been graced by a soaring neighbor on its northern edge.

The activity around Public Square also touched the northwest quadrant. In July 1988 the Jacobses bought the 1 and 33 Public Square buildings for approximately $20 million. At about the same time, Ameritrust Corporation officials had announced that they were selling their East Ninth Street headquarters to the Jacobs firm for $44 million, reportedly with the intention to occupy space in a rumored 60-story building to be built on the Square. The sale of their former home to the Jacobs brothers seemed to confirm that the brothers' new Public Square holding would be the site for the Ameritrust venture.

Once again, Public Square seemed to be on the verge of another exciting development. The momentum that the East Ninth Street corridor had gained as the city's financial district in the previous two decades was passing, as businesses began to express more interest in Public Square. As one real estate official said, "There is life after 9th and Euclid. People had serious doubts about that for a long time." The city's main park was where attention was being focused.

A month after the Jacobses bought the former Marshall and Public Square buildings, they revealed a plan for a 60-story office and hotel complex, which would lay claim to the title of the city's tallest, making Society Tower's reign a brief one. Ameritrust Corporation would indeed be the prime tenant, and accordingly the structure would be named the Ameritrust Center. The CEO of Ameritrust said the company was "delighted to be a major player in the final phase of the renaissance of Public Square."

Area residents were buzzing with talk of the proposed edifice. Writers in *The Plain Dealer*, for instance, referred to the plans for both towers --Society and Ameritrust--as symbols of a decade-long boom unprecedented in Cleveland history. Elsewhere downtown other development projects were moving ahead. The Gateway complex, while still on the drawing boards, was promising to bring new excitement to Indians'

The proposed Ameritrust Building, which would have risen just off the northwest quadrant and become the city's tallest structure, was stymied by bank consolidation. Instead of this dynamic skyscraper, the Square plays host to a parking lot. *(Ameritrust Corporation, Jim Toman Collection)*

and Cavs' fans and to the city. The Flats by this time had become a popular entertainment draw with its bars, nightclubs, and restaurants. Clevelanders had also worked hard to secure the Rock and Roll Hall of Fame and Museum for the lakefront, a development that many hoped would make Cleveland a tourist destination. Playhouse Square had jumped to life once again. By 1988, three of its theaters--the Ohio, State, and Palace--had been refurbished and were producing a full and varied menu of dramatic morsels. Back on the Square, the long-delayed plans to upgrade the neglected and obsolete Union Terminal station were once again heating up.

The Ameritrust Center would be another jewel in this glittering renaissance. The $400 million (later projected to be $357 million) structure was actually being designed as three distinct components: a Hyatt Regency Hotel, a separate headquarters building for Ameritrust, and a 60-story office tower. The architects, Kohn Pedersen Fox Associates of New York City, announced that the hotel portion was to face Public Square and include a 12-story atrium, a 12,000 square foot main ballroom, banquet and meeting rooms, two restaurants, and 484 guest rooms. The Ameritrust segment would face Superior Avenue. Rising above the 14-story hotel segment, a "dynamic futuristic tower" of curved, steel-blue glass would "thrust a dazzling new image of the city into the sky." Contrasting with the blue glass, a buff-colored granite skin would grace the rest of the building's exterior. At the top would be a stainless steel cap. The rounded portion of the structure would face the city's most famous landmark. The Ameritrust Center promised to complete the architectural enclosure of Public Square. Four gigantic skyscrapers, each adjacent to one of the four quadrants and each with a distinctively different stylistic flare to it, would dramatically overshadow the city green, proud sentinels standing guard over the civic center of northeast Ohio.

To make way for the Ameritrust Tower, demolition on the Marshall and Public Square buildings (1 and 33 Public Square) began in 1990. The view is from the southwest quadrant of the Square. *(Jim Toman photo)*

Demolition for the proposed Ameritrust edifice followed shortly after the Jacobses' announcement, within a month turning the project site just off the northwest quadrant into a heap of twisted metal and bricks. Originally construction was supposed to begin on January 1, 1991, but soon problems emerged, and in December 1990 the City approved the project site for a 144-space parking lot despite the objections of its own Fine Arts Advisory Committee. That group and other critics expressed disappointment that on such an important site in Cleveland, the City would allow a parking lot. Administration officials countered that not only was the parking lot a temporary reality there, but that given the slowdown of the economy, there were few options. And after all, a paved parking lot was preferable to a debris field.

The bombshell announcement that ultimately spelled the project's ruin came when Society Corporation announced its takeover of Ameritrust in September 1991. Part of the consolidation that dominated the banking industry in the last two decades of the 20th century, Society's purchase created a new company with assets that made it the largest bank in Cleveland and the 24th largest in the country. Portrayed in the media as a merger that solidified both banking institutions, the move then left the Ameritrust Center without a primary tenant. Although spokespeople for the Jacobs Group and the city administration were hesitant to call the proposed edifice dead, the project's prospects without Ameritrust were nil. Although Society officials attempted to reassure the public that they would honor the commitment to occupy 400,000 square feet in the Ameritrust Center, the promises never came to fruition. Instead, the bank reached agreement with the Jacobs group to meet that commitment by leasing additional space in the only partially filled Society Tower.

The recession, which translated into a sluggish office market, then forced the Jacobs Group to push back the project's completion date first to 1993 and then to 1996. And then no further word was forthcoming. Unlike the Van Sweringen brothers whose massive office building project in the 1930s stood mostly empty for over a decade, today's bottom-line-oriented businessmen do not subscribe to the *Field of Dreams* belief that "If you build it, they will come." In 1999 parked cars and a striped-surface lot still mar the Public Square scene. The completion of the Square's architectural facade remains a dream.

The Ameritrust proposal was not the Square's only phantom project. The Stouffer Corporation in the early 1990s announced its intention to build a 362-room addition to its Tower City Plaza Hotel to the west of the hotel's existing banquet facility on Superior Avenue. That plan, however, was scrapped in 1998 by the Renaissance Hotels International, which became the new owner of the hotel when Stouffer's left the hotel business. Another potential project included a 30-story office tower to be constructed at the intersection of Huron Road and Ontario Street and connected to the Landmark Office Buildings. That structure would have completed the Van Sweringens' original concept for their union station complex, but a glut in downtown office space kept the plans on paper only. Downtown Cleveland also passed by another opportunity for a subway. The Greater Cleveland Regional Transit Authority had proposed linking Public Square with University Circle via a light rail line along Euclid Avenue, with the section between East 18th Street and Public Square operated in subway. That plan was abandoned in 1995 when Mayor Michael White objected to the costs that it would entail and urged the transit planners to develop a less costly alternative.

While the Society and Ameritrust buildings may have focused many Clevelanders' attention again on Public Square, they were still no match for the interest and affection local residents felt for the Terminal Tower complex, which celebrated its 50th birthday in 1980. The grand old building's birthday party lasted ten days.

THE SQUARE'S TALLEST TOWERS

TERMINAL TOWER

YEAR CONSTRUCTION BEGAN	1923
YEAR OPENED	1927
NUMBER OF FLOORS	52
DEPTH OF FOUNDATION	200 feet
HEIGHT	708 feet
HEIGHT INCLUDING FLAGPOLE	763 feet
SQUARE FEET OF SPACE	610,000
OBSERVATION DECK	42nd floor

BP BUILDING

ORIGINAL NAME	Standard Oil Building
YEAR CONSTRUCTION BEGAN	982
YEAR OPENED	1985
NUMBER OF FLOORS	45
DEPTH OF FOUNDATION	240 feet
HEIGHT	653 feet
SQUARE FEET OF SPACE	1,200,000

KEY TOWER

ORIGINAL NAME	Society Tower
YEAR CONSTRUCTION BEGAN	1989
YEAR OPENED	1991
NUMBER OF FLOORS	57
DEPTH OF FOUNDATION	215 feet
HEIGHT	888 feet
HEIGHT INCLUDING SPIRE	948 feet
SQUARE FEET OF SPACE	1,410,000

The festivities began with a general open house, and Clevelanders were invited to revisit the place which had been so central to their downtown adventures. The front of the Terminal Tower was festooned with colorful banners, inside the stately portico Tower souvenirs were plentiful, and an art exhibit added spice to the concourse level. For the occasion the observation deck was opened to the public. During the week more colorful events were scheduled, too.

One of those events featured a re-creation of the 1938 baseball throw from the top of the Terminal Tower. This time, it involved a softball dropped by Ted Stepien, owner of the Cleveland Competitors professional softball team, to members of the team waiting at ground level. Approximately 5,000 onlookers watched the sunny mid-day event. Stepien was scheduled to toss six balls. Unfortunately, the first four throws were errant. The first hit a car on Superior Avenue, and the second, third, and fourth hit spectators, one breaking the wrist of a woman who was shielding her eyes from the sun's glare. The fifth toss was snared by a member of the team. The mission achieved, and in response to the unforeseen consequences of the first four throws, the sixth toss was canceled.

Another stunt later in the week also went awry. A professional stuntman named William R. DeRoyer was hired to conduct a rope-guided descent down the face of the Tower to its base. All went well on the first part of the drop. Then, when DeRoyer reached the 18th floor, his brakes failed and he flipped upside down and dangled helplessly above the pavement. Fortunately, he was able to recover, and he made the final part of the downward journey without further incident. The Terminal Tower was reportedly the tallest building ever featured in a rope descent.

Three members of the Cleveland Competitors professional softball team move into position to snag balls dropped from the 52nd floor of the Terminal Tower by team owner Ted Stepien. It was part of the 50th birthday celebration for the complex. *(Cleveland* Press *Collection of the Cleveland State University Libraries)*

Banners drape the entranceway to the Tower's portico in 1980 to commemorate the Cleveland Union Terminal complex's 50th birthday. The banners heralded a week of festive activities for Greater Clevelanders. *(JimToman photo)*

Onlookers were also treated to a stunning fireworks display as the week's celebration came to a close, following a party in the Square attended by some 5,000 Greater Clevelanders. For the entire ten-day event, sponsors estimated that approximately 200,000 went downtown to pay tribute to the city's most famous landmark.

As the decade of the 1980s proceeded, more substantial plans for the Tower complex began to take shape. In 1972, Sheldon B. Guren, chief of U.S. Realty Investments, then the owner of the Terminal Tower, had proposed a $350 million plan to create a "mini-city" surrounding the Tower. It was to include a 1,000-room hotel, two or three office buildings, terraced apartments overlooking the Cuyahoga River, and a 6,500-car underground parking garage. He also proposed combining the rapid transit station with the remaining railroad facilities. The U. S. Realty plan did not materialize, largely stymied by conflicts over who would be responsible for the repair to the bridge structures that carried traffic over the subterranean terminal concourses. Then in 1980 Forest City Enterprises, Inc. bought a 50% interest in the complex. By 1983, Forest City had acquired the entire office and station portions of the complex, later also adding the former main U.S. Post Office building. Forest City then worked with RTKL Architects, Inc. of Dallas to revise the original plans to include carving a shopping mall out of the old station area, renovating the existing office buildings, and adding two new office buildings and a hotel.

Cleveland won the first state and federal grants for the project in 1982, but the financing did not solidify until January 1986, when six local financial institutions provided a $59 million loan to Forest City. Before any construction took place on the complex itself, the bridge structures which carried Huron Road, Prospect Avenue, and West Second and West Third streets over the station had to be rebuilt to stop rain water runoff from seeping into the complex below. Actual construction on the project itself did not take place until 1988. When it did, it included results much more visible than the bridge repairs. Two new office towers were built, a new Skylight Office Tower and a combined Ritz-Carlton hotel and office building, both rising from foundations originally put down by the Van Sweringens but canceled by the Depression. The old postal facility was renovated into the new home of the M.K. Ferguson Company. Additional below-ground parking was squeezed into the old railroad platform area, and a new rapid transit station was built uniting all three rail rapid lines in one part of the facility. The most spectacular part of the redevelopment, however, was the total transformation of the historic Union Terminal into a retail haven. In the process, the two traction concourses disappeared, a second level of stores was squeezed in at Public Square level, a new skylighted plaza was added immediately behind the Terminal Tower building, and the roof of the old steam concourse was raised and replaced with a barrel-vaulted skylight, giving that section of the

The Van Sweringen dream for the Cleveland Union Terminal development was not finished during their lifetimes. For more than 50 years the clerestory above the steam concourse remained without office towers on either side (top). The Tower City project recreated a new skylight and built the long-missing towers (below). *(Jim Toman photos)*

mall three levels of shopping space. Each of the skylighted areas was furnished with fountains, the one in the former steam concourse spurting in synchronization with classical music that fitted the classy layout. Altogether the shopping mall provided space for 110 outlets and returned first-run movie going to downtown after an absence of 15 years. Preserving as much of the old as was practical, and adding the new in ways sensitive to the historic character of the venerable landmark, Tower City Center, at an estimated price tag of $400 million, became an instant hit with Clevelanders.

When Tower City opened in March 1990, thousands of Clevelanders turned out to see the newly remodeled area. While only about 60% of the 110 stores and six of the 11 movie screens were in operation and open to the public, eager Clevelanders gathered to see The Avenue--the retail, dining, and entertainment component of the complex. Opening festivities included speeches by local dignitaries, hundreds of balloons and banners, Disney characters, music, and other activities. Many of those in attendance were impressed with the complex and asserted that they would shop there more often. The Avenue reminded some observers of the draw that downtown retailers had on the public earlier in the century, when families would trek to Public Square for holidays and special occasions. But to other more skeptical observers, Tower City's arrival on the downtown shopping scene at a time when the economy was in recession raised the specter that the costly venture might ultimately fail. Time would seem to have proved those skeptics wrong.

Tower City has been one of the most consistently successful projects in Forest City's commercial portfolio. Retail occupancy has been strong since it opened, and officials have spoken about expanding the complex in the near future. The recent opening of the Hard Rock Cafe and stores like J. Crew has solidified the complex as an entertainment-based and high-end retail venue. Forest City officials have spoken of honoring the Van Sweringen vision by creating a constantly impressive project that improves upon itself so as not cheapen the brothers' legacy. Tower City officials see the center not just as a retail mecca, but also as a multi-dimensional people place, one that hosts small concerts, fashion shows, and rallies (like the one held to begin the countdown to the Browns' August 1999 kick-off).

The existing Tower City Center represents but the first phase of a much larger development. Phase II plans entail spreading Tower City south of Huron Road to the Cuyahoga River. The idea is to expand the complex with a "critical mass" at its heart--a core of retail, civic, and entertainment-based activity--centered in and around Tower City. In addition, Forest City planners also hope that the peninsula just west of the river can be converted to high-density residential use.

When Tower City opened, it helped the adjoining department store, which was struggling for survival against the draw of suburban shopping malls. The Dillard family and Edward DeBartolo, a developer of suburban shopping complexes, bought the Higbee Company in 1987 for $165 million, and promised to maintain the Higbee name. By August 1992, however, the Dillard name had replaced the Higbee moniker on the store's Public Square frontage. There were also rumors that the store's historic place as a part of the Terminal Tower complex was in jeopardy. Local chatter had DeBartolo negotiating to sell the building to an out-of-state investment group, which might have spelled doom for the Tower City anchor. In a move designed to keep Dillard's at 100 Public Square, Forest City Enterprises Inc., the owner of Tower City, purchased 50% of

The skylight concourse of Tower City center has become one of the city's most popular milling areas much as the steam concourse had been in years past. "I'll meet you at the fountain," has become a familiar refrain during the 1990s. *(Jim Toman photo)*

the building, assuring that the department store would remain at the corner of Ontario Street and Public Square at least until 2000.

At the same time, other retailers along Euclid Avenue were struggling to stay afloat. Some said that Tower City's success ultimately contributed to the shabby state of the avenue's retail strip. While the reality was much more complex, many believed that the glitter of The Avenue drew shoppers away from May's. On October 16, 1992, May Company officials announced that despite their attempts to keep the store viable, the 25% drop in sales during the three previous years, among other reasons, made it impossible to keep the flagship store open. An earlier plan to link the Higbee store with the May's store via a pedestrian bridge across Ontario Street might have bolstered May's position, but though approved by city planners, the bridge project was abandoned when federal Urban Development Action Grant (UDAG) funds dried up in 1989.

Not only did the May Company chain decide to close its Cleveland flagship store, it also determined that it would give the company's presence in the Cleveland area a new name, transferring the properties to its Kaufmann division. With the announcement, Cleveland Mayor Michael White journeyed to the Steel City to try to convince company leaders not to abandon their Public Square location. In the end, the efforts proved unsuccessful, as the downtown May Company closed on January 31, 1993.

The Tower City development as viewed from the Cuyahoga River also shows where Phase II of the complex would take place. The Sherwin-Williams facility is in the foreground. *(Jim Toman photo)*

Many Clevelanders, who had grown up with the department store on the Square, expressed frustration and even grief at the news of May Company's closing. Since 1899 the department store had been a fixture at the heart of the city. The May Company had been a pioneer in what had become the annual holiday decorations of the Square, and for decades had drawn thousands of shoppers downtown during the holiday season to take in "the magic of Christmas at May's." They marveled at May's festive window displays and interior decorations, visited Santa, and also enjoyed the Square's holiday lights. May Company's shiny terra cotta exterior was as much a part of Cleveland as the Terminal Tower or the Browns. Whether it was a place to shop on the weekends, or to buy back-to-school clothes, or to partake in holiday festivities, for 92 years the May Company was one of the most popular places to shop in downtown Cleveland.

So it was that during the last two decades of the millennium Public Square retail shopping met with mixed results. Tower City and Dillard's attracted people to the town green, but May Company's closing left a void on lower Euclid Avenue that would further accelerate that once busy thoroughfare's decline. The avenue sustained a further blow when the F. W. Woolworth store, a couple doors east of May's and the last of downtown's "variety" stores, closed in 1998.

The end of the decade brought a few more physical changes to the city center. In 1997 the first piece of Tower City Center's "Phase II" got underway. The federal government, searching for space to build a new courtroom tower, selected a site south of Huron Road at Superior Avenue, just across from West Ninth Street. Construction on the 24-story, $180 million project began in 1997, with completion expected in 2001. The new court tower and the Lausche State Office Building will be connected to The Avenue by means of an indoor walkway, similar to the one that connects it with Gateway. In effect, the connector will bring workers from the West Sixth and West Ninth street buildings to Public Square,

The familiar sign that welcomed people to the department store at 100 Public Square became a thing of the past in 1992, when the Higbee Company became Dillard's. By this time, less than half the building was still devoted to retail space. *(Jack Muslovski photo)*

contributing to the "critical mass" that Tower City planners envision as the key to the entire Phase II blueprint.

In 1998-1999 some "critical" attention was also given to one of the Square's oldest fixtures. The county commisioners were determined that the figures on the Soldiers and Sailors monument would get their weapons back. Over the years some of the bronze swords and other accoutrements of battle that belonged to the monument's four outdoor sculptures had been stolen--one by a man who also took rows of bronze spikes and sold them for scrap. At a cost of $315,000 the statuary groups, as well as the figure of Liberty atop the central pedestal, were completely restored.

Public Square's final architectural change of the century interestingly involved its oldest institution, the Old Stone Church. In 1995, to mark its 175th anniversary on Public Square, members of the congregation committed themselves to undertake a comprehensive restoration of their historic place of worship. The building's exterior was thoroughly cleaned in 1998, and on April 29, 1999, Public Square pedestrians watched in fascination as workers battled a windy day to position a new steeple atop the landmark church's east tower. Surmounted by an 8.8-foot stainless steel cross and rising 209 feet above Public Square, the aluminum steeple duplicates the earlier one that had been damaged by fire in 1884 and subsequently removed. The restored church gives comforting reassurance that in a century that witnessed so much change, some things endure.

Another enduring reality was Public Square's position as the center of community life. In the final two decades of the century special events there increased both in number and in their ability to draw people to the town center. Holiday tree-lightings on the Square continued throughout the last two decades of the 20th century, but the nature of the holiday displays became increasingly extravagant. Instead of just tree lightings, officials decided to expand the lights to include Square-wide displays. In 1984, Ohio Governor Paul Celeste flipped the ceremonial switch that bathed the city's park in blue, green, and white lights. Following the 37th annual holiday lighting ceremony (the tradition had been

As the years have passed and buildings have come and gone, one of the structures that has been a constant on the Square is the Old Stone Church. In 1999, a new aluminum steeple was installed on the historic church. *(Greg Deegan photo)*

interrupted by the Second World War years), fireworks were launched from behind the Terminal Tower to the delight of the estimated 6,000 people who had convened on Public Square to partake in the festivities.

The next year, city planners added a new wrinkle. They had workers install holiday lights around a Care Bears theme. Care Bears were the product of the American Greetings Corporation, a company headquartered in Cleveland, and they had become popular cartoon and greeting card characters. So the City decided to adorn the buildings that surrounded the Square with bears, and city officials explained that their presence helped to remind Clevelanders of the close bond between the commercial and civic renaissance that was taking place. The city even dubbed the Square Care-A-Lot Square for the month of December, a move some critics called a blatant sell-out to commercial interests. The Care Bears were a short-lived tradition. They were forced into hibernation in 1988 and replaced by "The Twinkling Kingdom of Cleveland" theme, but people continued to flock to the Square to take in the light displays.

By the 1990s, city planners had expanded the holiday displays and activities. They ordered a skating rink installed on the Terminal quadrant, impressed crowds with fireworks, and added entertainment. In 1993, the festivities were popular enough to draw an estimated 75,000 people to the Square to watch Santa Claus arrive amid fireworks that were attached to wires above the crowd. Showers of red and green stars fell upon the observers, and they were treated to a 24-foot-tall snowman on the northeast quadrant, a three-ring circus featuring Santa as ringmaster on the northwest quadrant, and a 30-foot lighted tree in the atrium of the BP Building. For the Bicentennial Homecoming Holiday Lighting ceremony in 1996, 55,000 showed up to enjoy festivities that included Santa Claus; Slider, the Cleveland Indians' mascot; dance performances by local residents; and a fireworks display. For the 1998 holidays, the Terminal Tower's normal golden hue was replaced with the Yule season's green and red.

New Year's Eve also drew people to the city's green during this period. The tradition began in the early 1980s at Playhouse Square and featured such things there as a nutcracker climbing the wall of the Halle Building to mark the countdown to the new year. In 1987, the event moved to Public Square and drew thousands to celebrate the new year's arrival in a distinctively Cleveland style. Instead of having an object drop to symbolize the passage of another year, a format which organizers said was too closely associated with New York City's Times Square, Clevelanders tried out other ways to ring in the next year. In 1989, some 4,000 people gathered to watch a pyrotechnic countdown that was fixed to a construction crane. The numbers of the last ten seconds, about 200 feet above Superior Avenue, blazed as the seconds counted down. Below, some onlookers broke out their private stocks of alcohol and cheered, even though the event was dubbed a non-alcohol affair. In 1994, about 5,000 attendees were treated to a rising logo--the Gateway symbol--which was hoisted to a crane in celebration of the new Jacobs Field that had opened that year. On the last day of 1995, about 7,000 people came to the Square to welcome in the new year with yet another logo. As the city was celebrating its upcoming bicentennial year, people watched the 7-by-7-foot Cleveland bicentennial logo hoisted up the front of

During the 1990s, on the southwest quadrant, a skaters' rink was installed as an extra attraction for Public Square holiday goers. The official city Christmas tree is in the background. *(Jim Toman photo)*

the Terminal Tower to the structure's 34th floor. Although organizers had hoped for a larger crowd, the people that did attend enjoyed the spectacle and were also treated to an after-midnight fireworks display.

Public Square not only hosted people for end-of-the-year festivities, but for summertime activities as well. On July 3, 1990, to mark the 60th anniversary of the Terminal Tower, the Cleveland Orchestra performed its first ever Public Square concert from a stage in front of the Terminal's portico. A crowd of 85,000 jammed the Square for the performance and the fireworks program which followed. In 1991 the Square again welcomed Clevelanders to a concert by the Cleveland Orchestra, replete with lasers, pyrotechnics, and fireworks synchronized with music. The lasers were projected onto the Terminal Tower, and the orchestra paid a classical tribute to the Rock and Roll Hall of Fame. The downtown orchestra concert became a summer tradition during the 1990s. The concerts typically drew more than 65,000 people to the town green. In 1995, not even rain could keep 75,000 people from the city's park. The concert, however, was not always held at the Square. In 1994, it took place in Jacobs Field, and in 1996 the orchestra performed in the Flats as part of the city's bicentennial celebration. The orchestra's tenth anniversay downtown concert in 1999 drew 65,000 to the Square despite a heat index of 103°.

When the Cleveland Orchestra performed on the Square in the 1990s, it did so to rave reviews. The lighted portico of the Terminal Tower was the backdrop and gave the Orchestra exposure to Clevelanders who might not have made it to Severance Hall or Blossom Music Center. *(Roger Mastroianni photo, Cleveland Orchestra Collection)*

Hollywood rolled into town for another holiday-related affair on the Square in 1983. MGM converted Public Square into a movie set for the film, *The Christmas Story*, which was set in the 1940s. Replete with floats, antique cars, toy soldiers, and clowns, the dramatization drew hundreds of onlookers and hopeful extras to the shoot. The movie company did an admirable job of recreating the town hub of the 1940s, with Higbee Co. decorations and window displays reminiscent of another era.

To celebrate the rejuvenation of civic life downtown, area groups decided during this period to establish another annual festival. Started in summer 1983, planners called it Celebration Square to Square. Along a Euclid Avenue that was closed to traffic from Public Square to Playhouse Square, retailers, restauranteurs, entertainers, and civic groups set up stations. The event, planned by the Growth Association's Business Council, Playhouse Square Foundation, Public Square merchants, Tower City Center, the City of Cleveland, and other groups, turned the downtown area along Euclid into a giant pedestrian mall. Attendees were treated to parades, dancers, food, music, games, and shopping. Such events as a beer slide, sponsored by Christian Schmidt Brewing Company; performances by stars such as Steve Allen and Roberta Flack at the theaters; Parties in the Park; and one-mile fitness runs drew area residents to the summer festivities.

Organizers said they hoped to highlight what downtown Cleveland had to offer in order to draw people back to the city. The co-chairwoman of the 1984 party said she hoped thousands of residents would come to celebrate in the one neighborhood that belonged to everyone: the downtown. The first year was deemed a success as sponsors estimated that as many as 70,000 people attended. The Square to Square event was repeated for several years.

While a variety of activities drew people to the city's hub, conspicuously absent for decades from Public Square were events relating to the local sports scene. Cleveland professional sports teams

Among the continuing downtown perennial favorites was the St. Patrick's Day parade. Clevelanders always turned out in huge numbers to put on the green. Here the parade winds from the Square past the reviewing stand on Superior Avenue. *(Cleveland* Press *Collection of the Cleveland State University Libraries)*

during the decades before the 1980s mirrored the sluggish city. The last celebration for the Indians took place in 1954 when they captured the American League pennant, and the last real hurrah for the Browns was the team's 1964 league championship victory over the Baltimore Colts, but even then there were no great downtown gatherings to honor the victors. The Cavaliers, Barons, Force, and other teams never captured the city's attention as had the football and baseball teams, and neither did they celebrate much in the way of victories. So for almost 50 years, Public Square lay dormant as a place for celebrating sports accomplishments.

That changed in 1995, when the Cleveland Indians dramatically captured the American League pennant. Interest in the team, bolstered by the sad Browns' chapter then being written on the lakefront, brought an enthusiasm to the city that had been long absent. With come-from-behind victories, sell-out crowds, and exciting baseball players such as Albert Belle, Eddie Murray, and Kenny Lofton leading the way, the Indians cruised to 100 wins, only to fall short in the World Series against the Atlanta Braves. Before the Series, team members were treated to a Public Square send-off rally, and though they did not clinch the Series championship, when they returned to the city, they received heroes' welcomes at a sun-drenched party on Public Square. Attended by tens of thousands of screaming fans, the American League champions thanked the crowd for its enthusiastic support. Sitting on a platform above the crowd, the players joked, danced, and created a festive atmosphere. In 1997 the Indians again made it to the World Series, only losing the grand prize in extra innnings in the seventh game, and again the city paid tribute to the team with a giant celebration.

Tribe fever dominated Public Square in October 1995 as thousands of Indians fans gathered to cheer on the team for making it to its first World Series appearance in 41 years. Old Stone Church and the Society for Savings Building are in the background. *(Ron Kuntz photo)*

Indians mascot Slider was joined by pitcher Orel Hershiser on Public Square during a giant appreciation rally for the Tribe after its valiant effort in the 1997 World Series. The Renaissance Cleveland Hotel is in the background. *(Ron Kuntz photo)*

Football too shared in the Public Square spotlight. Following the painful relocation of the city's National Football League team to Baltimore following the 1995 season, Clevelanders for three years eagerly awaited the promised return of the Browns. The excitement climaxed on the weekend of August 14, 1999, when the team's brand new stadium on the lakefront opened for public tours which drew an estimated 100,000 to the state-of-the-art facility. On August 20, the City hosted a Euclid Avenue parade to welcome officially the reconstituted Browns. A crowd of about 30,000 lined Euclid Avenue and filled the Square for a rally in which the fans enthusiastically cheered on the team which was to make its home exhibition-game debut the next evening.

During the 1990s, the city, and the Square, had again come alive for sports.

As in the past, protesters, politicians, and demonstrators found a welcome mat at the city's hub, too. During the 1980 presidential campaign, Ronald Reagan addressed 4,000 supporters during a Public Square rally on a drizzly May 30. While he was downtown, his opponent, Jimmy Carter was wooing voters in Parma. In the 1988 campaign, Michael Dukakis also conducted a Public Square rally. While he was speaking in the southwest quadrant, however, Republican activists held a counter rally from the steps of the Soldiers and Sailors monument, and Pro-Life Democrats marched along Superior Avenue to protest the candidate's views on abortion. During the 1992 campaign, while George Bush took to the stump in suburban Strongsville, both Bill and Hillary Clinton spoke downtown. On August 21 Bill Clinton spoke to 6,000 from the steps of the Board of Education Building on East Sixth Street, while on October 27, a small but enthusiastic crowd of 3,500 cheered the future first lady on Public Square.

On the campaign trail in 1980, future President Ronald Reagan came to Public Square to rally supporters. By this time, the position for the speaker's rostrum on the Square had become well-established--in front of the Terminal Tower portico. *(Cleveland* Press *Collection of the Cleveland State University Libraries)*

Other kinds of civic discourse also made ample use of the Square. In August 1990 a group called Project Open Hand Inc. used the town green as a place to remind Clevelanders of the area's homeless. One of the organizers of the group erected a tent on the northwest quadrant and fasted for 40 days to publicize the cause. During that time, about ten other tents were put up around the Tom L. Johnson statue to support the group. By the 24th day, officials of the Parks, Recreation and Properties Department ordered all the tents removed from the Square except for the original demonstrator's because people in the demonstration were serving food and making the site a health hazard. In addition, city officials said that Public Square's sanitary conditions were suffering because of the number of people that had taken up temporary residence on the city's front lawn.

In another demonstration, this one during the Persian Gulf War in 1991, about a dozen anti-war protesters staged their "deaths" in Public Square as about 1,000 onlookers voiced their opposition to U.S. involvement in the war. The "die-in" members, who had smeared red paint on themselves and who dangled a stuffed effigy of then-President George Bush, dropped to the pavement in front of the BP America Building between Euclid and Superior avenues, blocking automobile and RTA bus traffic for two hours. After the protesters were ordered from that area, some took over Superior Avenue and blocked other intersections throughout the Square. In the end, they were forced to leave without further incident.

Controversy stirred in the city's central park over matters far less substantial than war, though. As construction workers were in the process of reworking the quadrants and improving their greenery, the city's chief construction inspector in charge of Public Square, Gus Callas, expressed frustration at the numbers of pigeons that seemed to be invading the area. Echoing decades-old concerns regarding the Square and the feathered creatures, he said the birds' waste was destroying the new red bricks and the newly cleaned statues. The pigeons, he told a *Plain Dealer* reporter, were "ruining it for other people who want to enjoy the square."

Winning more favor with Public Square birdwatchers were a pair of peregrine falcons, nicknamed Szell and Zenith, which made a home on a twelfth-floor ledge of the Terminal Tower. The pair's courtship was carefully monitored in the media, and Clevelanders took great pleasure in the 16 chicks they produced. In spring 1999 Clevelanders were also amazed to witness an aerial battle between Zenith and another female falcon who had made a vain attempt to win over the affections of Bullett, Szell's successor. The battle ended with Zenith triumphant, her competitor taking wing for safer surroundings than Public Square provided. Domestic peace was thus restored to the falcons' nest.

The 1990s brought a new vantage point for Public Square observers. For the first time in the city's history, one could look down upon the Terminal Tower. The view is from the top of Key Tower. *(Jim Toman photo)*

As public a space as the Square is, on occasion it has not been immune to the kind of human behavior usually relegated to more shadowy places. A disturbing incident on the Square took place on July 16, 1980. On that day witnesses reported seeing a woman in a fight with a few men near the fountain in the redeveloped northeast quadrant. About 40 bystanders were in the area and witnessed the altercation. A few people attempted to go to the aid of the woman, but the perpetrators warned them off. Before the police could respond, the woman was raped, but as the rapists then tried to flee the area, they were nabbed by police just arriving on the scene.

Thankfully, such events have been very rare in the history of the Square. Much more common are those of people of good will, who come to the city center to rally for various causes, ranging from AIDS awareness, to animal rights, to the legalization of marijuana, and to support both sides of the nation's long-divisive debate over abortion. Protesters, too, often find in the Square the most meaningful locale for advocating their cause to their fellow citizens. Serbian-Americans, for instance, in spring 1999 used the downtown park for a protracted protest against the NATO air campaign against their homeland. The central green has even beckoned modern-day pagans and witches, who on May Day (May 1) re-enact there the ancient rituals of their nature religions.

The last decades of the century brought many welcome changes to the Public Square landscape. But while the architecture enclosed the city green in an ever more urban perimeter, the physical changes seemed only to reinforce for the community the importance of the Square as civic ground zero. The tradition of the Square as the center of celebration and ceremony and as a forum for free speech gained force during the century's closing years. The number and variety of the events held there, as well as the size of the crowds who participated in them, give ample testimony that the heartbeat of Cleveland was steady and strong.

If those Clevelanders who celebrated the start of the century by watching the parade of primitive cars sputtering through the Square could have returned at the century's end, they would surely have been amazed by the grand structures that then surrounded it. But they would also have found the familiar--the Square still divided into four quadrants, and on the periphery, the Old Stone Church, the Society for Savings Building, the Soldiers and Sailors monument, and the Moses Cleaveland statue. As Clevelanders, it would not have taken them long to feel very much right at home.

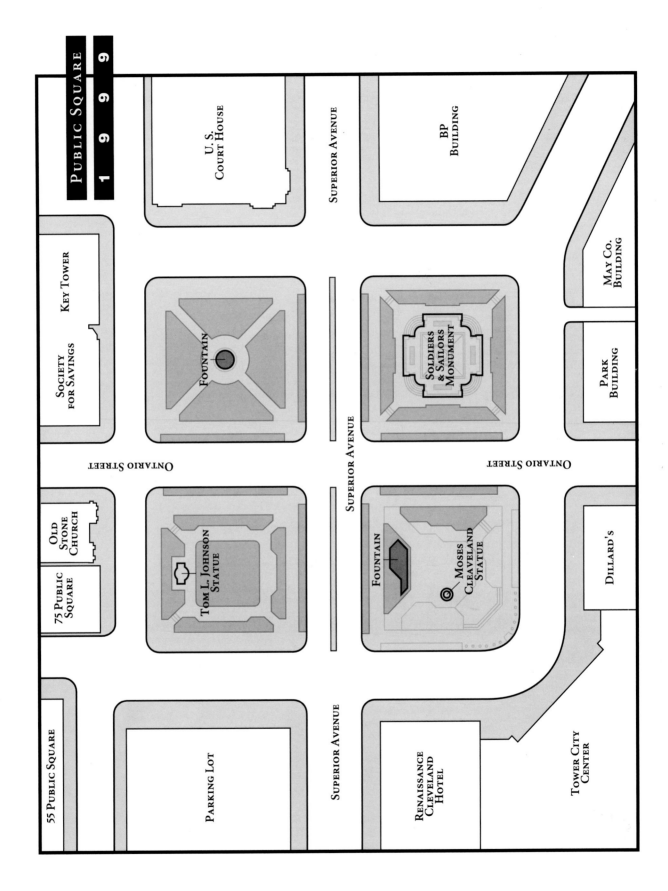

U. S.
COURT HOUSE

SUPERIOR AVENUE

BP
BUILDING

KEY TOWER

MAY CO.
BUILDING

SOCIETY
FOR SAVINGS

FOUNTAIN

SOLDIERS
& SAILORS
MONUMENT

PARK
BUILDING

ONTARIO STREET

SUPERIOR AVENUE

ONTARIO STREET

OLD
STONE
CHURCH

75 PUBLIC
SQUARE

TOM L. JOHNSON
STATUE

FOUNTAIN

MOSES
CLEAVELAND
STATUE

DILLARD'S

55 PUBLIC SQUARE

PARKING LOT

SUPERIOR AVENUE

RENAISSANCE
CLEVELAND
HOTEL

TOWER CITY
CENTER

Epilogue

Those hearty parade watchers on Public Square on January 1, 1900, would find the current appearance of Public Square amazing. A century brings many changes. Realizing this, any attempt to predict what the Public Square precinct will be like at the start of the 22nd century would be either an act of foolishness or hubris. Even trying to guess 50 years ahead, when the pace of technological change is so momentous, seems little more than fantasy.

As the 21st century dawns, much of downtown is changing. Recent emphasis on making Cleveland a tourist attraction has resulted in the final decade of the 20th century being a time when change downtown took the form of stadiums, arenas, museums, and hotel rooms. The Warehouse District and the Gateway Neighborhood began to blossom as residential neighborhoods. Major high rise office construction, on the other hand, slowed almost to a halt--not just in Cleveland but across the nation, influenced no doubt both by corporate downsizing and by the ease with which lap top computers, E-mail, the Internet, and cellular telephones have made business offices rather portable.

And yet the impetus to glance into the future is irresistible. And if that glance is not too forward looking, perhaps some sense of direction can be reasonably detected.

The Moses Cleaveland statue on Public Square is dwarfed by the soaring Tower. Both, however, are enduring symbols of the city. *(Greg Deegan photo)*

The future of the former May Company department store building is unsettled at century's end. The view is from the Society for Savings Building. *(Jim Toman photo)*

As the 20th century came to a close, citizens continued to think about the future of Public Square. In May 1998, Cleveland Tomorrow, an organization of chief executives of major area corporations, made a series of recommendations on downtown planning. Some of the major points of the group's report, called Civic Vision 2000 and Beyond, advocated further investment along the lakefront. Ideas included in the report were building a new aquarium and retail district west of East Ninth Street and a new downtown convention center, also possibly located near the lakefront.

Responding to the plan, representatives from about a half dozen local organizations were critical that it did not pay sufficient attention to the importance of open space and parks in maximizing the attractiveness of the lakefront and other downtown areas. Among other suggestions, their proposal echoed sentiments of Clevelanders past: to eliminate Ontario Street and Superior Avenue from bisecting Public Square. These advocates point out that this would result in the effective creation of Ohio's largest center city park and significantly add aesthetic beauty to the heart of the downtown area. Some even suggested that transforming the park in such way would make the area a draw for downtown living, perhaps creating new apartments in the vacant upper stories of the Dillard and May Company buildings.

Both structures have posed their own set of challenges and considerations. In 1999, the downtown Dillard's store had about a half million square feet of vacant space on its upper floors (the most recent abandonment was the 1990 closing of the once-popular Silver Grill on the tenth floor). Ideas of energizing the building have included both residential and retail-oriented plans, but as of 1999 nothing tangible has emerged. The problem with alternate uses for both Dillard's and its May Company counterpart is that both structures have very deep floor plates. This means that much space is in the "deep core" of the buildings, far from windows. In order to make the structures viable for residential use, for instance, plans would have to include creating atriums with skylights, a very expensive proposition.

Plans to reconfigure the Square are problematic, for they impact established traffic patterns in and through the city center. RTA operates 65 of its 100 bus routes through the city's green, and traffic counts reveal that Superior Avenue carries some 17,000 vehicles daily and Ontario another 9,000. Advocates of making the Square more park-like conceded that in order for the traffic question to be addressed adequately, Public Square's traffic plans would have to be tied more closely to the Euclid Corridor project that RTA hopes to launch early in the new century.

The proponents of the current Euclid Corridor project, a replacement for the abandoned Dual-Hub subway and light rail line, hope to revitalize Euclid Avenue from Public Square to University Circle in several ways. The centerpiece of the plan is to redirect most automobile traffic away from Euclid Avenue by reducing the number of lanes available to private vehicles. A reserved median strip would be set aside for a non-polluting trackless trolley line, and the avenue would become greener with the addition of tree-lined sidewalks and trees in the center median. The hope is that these changes would then create a climate conducive to more residential development. Changes in Euclid Avenue would, of course, also mean changes for the Square.

The 55 Public Square Building, 75 Public Square Building, Old Stone Church, Society for Savings Building, and Key Tower line the northern edge of the Square. *(Greg Deegan photo)*

Perhaps the most successful treatment of the Square comes in the way the Terminal Tower group enfolds the southwest quadrant. That quadrant is also the location for most of the Square events. *(Jim Toman photo)*

And so the debate about the future of Public Square continues. On one side are those who seek to remake the city's green into a serene pastoral preserve, believing that a tree-filled park would create a refuge in the heart of a pulsating city. On the other are those who believe that the traffic through the Square promotes a certain vibrancy to the heart of the city. Whatever the viewpoint, the discussion about the Square ultimately has been one about the nature of the city itself. So, it is likely that in the future, as in the past, Clevelanders will continue to debate any alterations to the Square. It is a essentially a civic discourse about the town's character.

There are, of course, more immediately pragmatic concerns, too. What can be done with the cavernous May Company Building? Can it be converted to some other use, or will it eventually meet the wrecker's ball? Can downtown Cleveland hang on to its one remaining department store? What about the parking lot next to the northwest quadrant? How much longer will the promise of that key space go unfulfilled? Will the dream of surrounding the Square with four towers ever come true?

Public Square has been a microcosm of Cleveland throughout the years. It has faithfully served Clevelanders both as a place of respite and relaxation as well as a forum for civic celebration and mourning. The city's park has hosted protests, demonstrations, and rallies. Its fortunes and those of the broader city have been intertwined.

Public Square throughout the 20th century has remained the centerpiece of downtown, but it has done so not as a result of coordinated planning by elected officials. Rather the face of the

Square has changed as commercial interests and private groups in the city have seen fit to change it. That pattern is likely to hold true for the indefinite future. The public purse is unlikely to overflow any time soon.

But as the Ohio Supreme Court pointed out, Public Square really belongs to the people, not to any specific governmental unit. Over the years citizens have diligently protected the open space of the Square. Numerous plans that would have violated the original design of Public Square have been met with intense opposition, whether those originated with governmental or commercial interests. The "vox populi" has sounded loud and clear when the traditional layout of the Square has been threatened. That too is unlikely to change.

During the 20th century much of downtown has been transformed. The Flats became the place for Clevelanders to party, East Ninth Street emerged into the town's financial center, Gateway became the home for professional sports in Cleveland, the lakefront developed into a museum and tourist center, and the Warehouse District turned into a residential area for young professionals. All of that represented major change.

Unchanged, though, was what was at the heart of it all. Public Square remained the city green, the civic center, the downtown park. It remained what it always was--the heart of Cleveland. If one were to wager about the city at the dawn of the next century, one might feel confident of at least this: that the public space of Public Square will continue to be public space, and that it will continue to be for the people the real heart of the city.

OTHER CLEVELAND BOOKS AVAILABLE AT YOUR BOOKSTORE OR BY MAIL FROM CLEVELAND LANDMARKS PRESS, INC.

CLEVELAND STADIUM: THE LAST CHAPTER, a history of the old Cleveland Municipal Stadium from planning through demolition; soft cover, 135 pages, 140 illustrations, $24.50 (+$3.50 shipping)

CLEVELAND TRANSIT THROUGH THE YEARS, a review of major transit events in Cleveland during the 20th century; soft cover, 48 pages, 45 illustrations, $8.95 (+ $3.00 shipping)

FUMBLE! THE BROWNS, MODELL AND THE MOVE, an analysis of what went wrong for the Browns that led to their leaving in 1995; hard cover, 331 pages, 50 illustrations, $24.00 (+3.50 shipping)

CLEVELAND'S DYNAMIC TRANSIT HERITAGE, an illustrated review of Cleveland transit developments from horse car days through 1985; soft cover, 34 pages, 75 illustrations, $4.95 (+$3.00 shipping)

CLEVELAND'S TRANSIT VEHICLES, an illustrated description and roster of Cleveland's public transit equipment; hard cover, 288 pages, 142 illustrations, $47.00 (+4.00 shipping)

HORSE TRAILS TO REGIONAL RAILS, a complete history of public transit in Cleveland; hard cover, 376 pages, 332 illustrations, $49.00 (+ $4.00 shipping)

WHEN CLEVELAND HAD A SUBWAY, a photo essay on the streetcar subway on the lower deck of Detroit-Superior (Veterans Memorial) Bridge; soft cover, 48 pages, 45 illustrations, $8.95 (+ $3.00 shipping)

CLEVELAND LANDMARKS PRESS, INC.
13610 Shaker Boulevard, Suite 503
Cleveland, Ohio 44120-1592